THE NATION APPL[AUDS]
A BRILLIANT YOUNG WRITER . . .

PIGEON FEATHERS

and Other Stories

by John Updike

A Fawcett Crest Book

FAWCETT PUBLICATIONS, INC., GREENWICH, CONN.

MEMBER OF AMERICAN BOOK PUBLISHERS COUNCIL, INC.

A Fawcett Crest Book reprinted by arrangement with
Alfred A. Knopf, Inc.

PRINTING HISTORY
Six Alfred A. Knopf printings

An alternate selection of the Book-of-the-Month Club
• • • • •
Of these nineteen stories, seventeen were originally published in
The New Yorker. "Archangel" was first printed in *Big Table*; "The
Crow in the Woods" in *the Transatlantic Review*. The stories are
arranged in the order in which they were written.

Published by Fawcett World Library, 67 West 44th
Street, New York, New York 10036
Printed in the United States of America.

TO WILLIAM MAXWELL

In revenge, however, my memory of the past has closed the door against me more and more. I could have returned at first, had human beings allowed it, through an archway as wide as the span of heaven over the earth, but as I spurred myself on in my forced career, the opening narrowed and shrank behind me; I felt more comfortable in the world of men and fitted it better; the strong wind that blew after me out of my past began to slacken; today it is only a gentle puff of air that plays around my heels; and the opening in the distance, through which it comes and through which I once came myself, has grown so small that, even if my strength and my will power sufficed to get me back to it, I should have to scrape the very skin from my body to crawl through.

—KAFKA, "*A Report to an Academy*"

Contents

PIGEON
FEATHERS
and Other Stories

Walter Briggs

COMING BACK from Boston, Jack drove, his baby son slept in a Carry-Cot on the front seat beside him, and in the back seat Clare sang to their girl, Jo, age two.

"When the pie was open, the birds began to—?"

"King," the child said.

"Wasn't that a dainty dish, to set before the—?"

"King!"

"That's right."

"Sing birdy nose song."

"Sing birdy nose song? I don't know the birdy nose song. *You* sing the birdy nose song. How does it go?"

"How does go?"

"I'm asking you. Who sings you the birdy nose song? Did Miss Duni do that?"

Jo laughed at the old joke; "Miss Duni" was a phrase that had popped magically from her mouth one day. "Who's Miss Duni?" she asked now.

"*I* don't know who Miss Duni is. You're the one who knows Miss Duni. When did she teach you the birdy nose song?"

"Birdy nose, birdy nose, knock knock, knock," the little girl chanted lightly.

"What a *good* song! I wish Miss Duni would teach it to me."

"It's the second stanza of the blackbird song," Jack said. "Down came a blackbird and picked off her nose."

"I've *never* sung it to her," Clare vowed.

"But you know it. It's in your genes."

In ten minutes—the trip took fifty—the child fell asleep, and Clare eased this weight off her lap. Then, turning from a mother into a wife, she rested her chin on the back of the front seat, near Jack's shoulder, and breathed on the right side of his neck.

"Who did you like best at the party?" he asked.

"I don't know, really. It's hard. I'll say Langmuir, because he saw what I meant about Sherman Adams."

"Everybody saw what you meant; it's just that everybody saw it was stupid."

"It wasn't."

"Who's best," he asked her, "Langmuir or Foxy?" This game, Who's Best?, was one of their few devices for whiling away enforced time together. A poor game, it lacked the minimal element of competition needed to excite Jack.

"I suppose Langmuir," Clare said, after taking thought.

"Knifing poor old Foxy in the back. And he loves you so."

"He *is* kind; I hate myself. Uh—who's best, Foxy, or the boy with the cleft chin and the help-me eyes?"

"The boy with the help-me eyes," he promptly answered. "Oh he's awful. What *is* his name?"

"Crowley? Cra— Crackers?"

"Something like that. Graham Crackers. What was the name of the girl he was with with the big ears who was so lovely?"

"The poor thing, whatever makes her think she can wear those bobbly gold gypsy rings?"

"She's not ashamed of her ears. She's proud. She thinks they're grand. Which they are—a lovely girl. To think, I may never see her again."

"*Her* name had *o*'s in it."

"Orlando. Ooh-Ooh Orlando, the soap-bubble queen."

"Not quite."

The superhighway made a white pyramid in the headlights; the murmur of the motor sounded lopsided, and occasionally a whiff of gasoline haunted the car's interior. *Fuel pump,* he thought, and visualized jets of explosive fluid spraying the piping-hot metal. Pieces of dirt had always been getting into the fuel pump of his father's old Buick, and the car would flood and stall. "This car is going to start costing us money soon," he said, and got no response. She refused to hear anything of their trading it in, though they had owned it four years and had never quite adjusted to the color, Waterfall Blue. He glanced at the speedometer and said, "Twenty-three thousand miles it's travelled for us." He added, "Birdy nose, birdy nose, knock knock knock."

Clare laughed abruptly, at something she had thought of. "I know. What was the name of that fat man at Arrow Island who stayed the whole summer and played bridge every night and wore a droopy fisherman's hat?"

He laughed, too, at her recalling this man. The first three months of their married life, five years ago, had been spent at a Y.M.C.A. family camp on an island in a New Hampshire lake. Jack had worked as registrar, and his bride had run the camp store. "Walter," he began confidently. "Then something monosyllabic. He was always fishing down by that row of men's tents and was there when we got there and stayed after we left, to help them take the metal pier down." He could see everything about the man: his sly cat's smile, the peak of hair at the back of his head, his hemispherical stomach, his candy-striped T shirt and his crepe-soled shoes.

"Give me," Clare went on, "Mrs. Young's first name." Young, a chain-smoking blunderer, had been in charge of the camp; his wife was a short thick-necked woman with a square face and alert green eyes and, like so many wives of "good" men, a rather tart tongue. Once, she had called up from the mainland with an excursion of children, and Jack, overworked, had forgotten to tell the Dartmouth boy who ran the launch, and when she called an hour later, still waiting with these whiny children on the hot mainland, Jack had exclaimed into the faint telephone (the underwater cable was all but eaten away), "How ghastly!" After that, all summer, she called him How Gawstly. Coming into the office, she would rasp, "And how's good old How Gawstly?" and Jack would blush.

"Georgene," he said.

"Right," Clare said. "Now their two girls."

"One was Muffie, she was the tractable one. And the other—"

"*I* know."

"Wait. Muffie and—it kind of rhymed. Muffie and Toughie."

"Audrey. She had a chipped front tooth."

"*Very* good. Now let's think about that fat man. It began with *B*. Baines. Bodds. Byron. They went together, so you never thought of him as one name or the other but as both run together. Walter Buh, buh—isn't that maddening?"

"Byron sounds close. Remember he was so good at shuffleboard, and organized the tournaments every week?"

"He played cards at night, in the rec hall. I can just *see* him, sitting there, on a brown, steel, folding chair."

"Didn't he live the rest of the year in Florida?" she asked, laughing at the idea of a man spending his entire year in vacation spots, and laughing further because if you tried to imagine such a man, who could he be but lazy, complacent Walter Somebody?

"He used to sell plumbing equipment," Jack said with triumph. "He was retired." But this avenue, like the others, queerly failed to lead to the sanctum where the man's name was hidden. "I can remember their professions but not their names," he said, anxious to put in something for himself, for he felt his wife was getting ahead of him at this game. "I should remember them all," he went on. "I wrote all their names down on those damn cards."

"Yes, you should. Who was that girl who had to leave the island because she started throwing stones at people?"

"God, yes. Mentally disturbed, and *aw*fully good-looking. And never said anything."

"She used to stand under trees and brood."

"Oh, how Young worried with her! And that other Special Case, who was always coming back on the train, and said his brother in Springfield would pay, and the Y had this special fund he thought was all for him. . . ."

"He loved chess so. Checkers. I guess you tried to teach him chess."

"Everything you'd show him on the board, he'd say, 'Pretty neat,' or 'You're a mighty smart fella.' "

"And every time you'd say anything he'd sense you thought was funny, he'd laugh hysterically, that high laugh. He loved us, because we were nice to him."

"Robert—"

"*Roy*, darling; how could you forget Roy? And then there was Peg Grace."

"Peg, Grace. Those huge eyes."

"And that tiny long nose with the nostrils shaped like water wings," Clare said. "Now: tell me the name of her pasty-faced boy friend."

"With the waxy blond hair. Lord. I can't con*ceiv*ably hope to remember his name. He was only there a week."

"I always remember him coming up from the lake after swimming. That long white body and then those tiny black bathing trunks: sexy. Oogh."

"He *was* white. But not unpleasant. In retrospect," Jack announced pompously, "I like them all, except the German kitchen boy with curly hair he thought was so cute and apoplectic cheeks."

"You didn't like him because he was always making eyes at me."

"Was he? Yes he was, now that I think. The thing I really had against him, though, was that he beat me so badly in the broad jump. Then the Peruvian beat him, happily."

"Escobar."

"*I* knew his name. He was always trying to play basketball with his head."

"And then Barbara, the gay divorcee."

"Walter Barbara. Walter, Ba, Be, Bi, Bo, Bu. He had a monstrous bill at the end of the summer."

But Clare was no longer waiting for the fat man. She danced ahead, calling into color vast faded tracts of that distant experience: the Italian family with all the empty beer cans, the tall deaf-mute who went around barefoot and punctured the skin of his foot on a chopped root in the east path, the fire hazard until those deadly August rains, the deer on the island that they never saw. The deer came over on the ice in the winter and the spring thaw trapped them. It made him jealous, her store of explicit memories—the mother at dusk calling "Beryl, Beryl," the gargantuan ice-cream cones the boys on Murray's crew served themselves—but she moved among her treasures so quickly and gave them so generously he had to laugh at each new face and scene offered him, because these were memories they had collected together and he was happy that they had discovered such a good game for the car just when he thought there were no more games for them. They reached the region of familiar roads, and he drove a long way around, to prolong the trip a minute.

Home, they carried the children to bed—Clare the tiny boy, as fragile as a paper construction, and Jack the heavy, flushed girl. As he lowered her into the crib, she opened her eyes in the darkness.

"Home," he told her.

"Whezouh dirt?" A new road was being bulldozed not far from their house, and she enjoyed being taken to see the mounds of earth.

"Dirt in the morning," Jack said, and Jo accepted this.

Downstairs, the two adults got the ginger ale out of the refrigerator and watched the midnight news on provincial television, Governor Furcolo and Archbishop Cushing looming above Khrushchev and Nasser, and went to bed hastily, against the children's morning rising. Clare fell asleep immediately, after her long day of entertaining them all.

Jack felt he had made an unsatisfactory showing. Their past

was so much more vivid to her presumably because it was
more precious. Something she had mentioned nagged him.
The German boy's making eyes at her. Slowly this led him
to remember how she had been, the green shorts and the
brown legs, holding his hand as in the mornings they walked
to breakfast from their cabin, along a lane that was two dusty
paths for the wheels of the jeep. Like the deaf-mute, Clare
had gone around barefoot, and she walked between the paths,
on a brand mane of weeds. Her hand, her height had seemed
so small, the fact of her waking him so strange. She always
heard the breakfast bell, though it rang far away. Their cabin
was far from the center of things; its only light had been a
candle. Each evening (except Thursday, when he played
right field for the staff softball team) in the half hour between
work and dinner, while she made the bed within, he had sat
outside on a wooden chair, reading in dwindling daylight
Don Quixote. It was all he had read that summer, but he had
read that, in half hours, every dusk, and in September cried
at the end, when Sancho pleads with his at last sane master
to rise from his deathbed and lead another quest, and perhaps
they shall find the Lady Dulcinea under some hedge, stripped
of her enchanted rags and as fine as any queen. All around
the cabin had stood white pines stretched to a cruel height
by long competition, and the cabin itself had no windows, but
broken screens. Pausing before the threshold, on earth littered
with needles and twigs, he unexpectedly found what he
wanted; he lifted himself on his elbow and called "Clare"
softly, knowing he wouldn't wake her, and said, "Briggs.
Walter Briggs."

The Persistence of Desire

PENNYPACKER'S OFFICE still smelled of linoleum, a clean, sad scent that seemed to lift from the checkerboard floor in squares of alternating intensity; this pattern had given Clyde as a boy a funny nervous feeling of intersection, and now he stood crisscrossed by a double sense of himself, his present identity extending down from Massachusetts to meet his disconsolate youth in Pennsylvania, projected upward from a distance of years. The enlarged, tinted photograph of a lake in the Canadian wilderness still covered one whole wall, and the walnut-stained chairs and benches continued their vague impersonation of the Shaker manner. The one new thing, set squarely on an orange end table, was a compact black clock constructed like a speedometer; it showed in Arabic numerals the present minute—1:28—and coiled invisibly in its works the two infinites of past and future. Clyde was early; the waiting room was empty. He sat down on a chair opposite the clock. Already it was 1:29, and while he watched, the digits slipped again: another drop into the brimming void. He glanced around for the comfort of a clock with a face and gracious, gradual hands. A stopped grandfather matched the other imitation antiques. He opened a magazine and immediately read, "Science reveals that the cells of the normal human body are replaced *in toto* every seven years."

The top half of a Dutch door at the other end of the room opened, and, framed in the square, Pennypacker's secretary turned the bright disc of her face toward him. "Mr. Behn?" she asked in a chiming voice. "Dr. Pennypacker will be back from lunch in a minute." She vanished backward into the maze of little rooms where Pennypacker, an eye, ear, nose, and throat man, had arranged his fabulous equipment. Through the bay window Clyde could see traffic, gayer in color than he remembered, hustle down Grand Avenue. On

17

the sidewalk, haltered girls identical in all but name with girls he had known strolled past in twos and threes. Small town perennials, they moved rather mournfully under their burdens of bloom. In the opposite direction packs of the opposite sex carried baseball mitts.

Clyde became so lonely watching his old street that when, with a sucking exclamation, the door from the vestibule opened, he looked up gratefully, certain that the person, this being his home town, would be a friend. When he saw who it was, though every cell in his body had been replaced since he had last seen her, his hands jerked in his lap and blood bounded against his skin.

"Clyde Behn," she pronounced, with a matronly and patronizing yet frightened finality, as if he were a child and these words the moral of a story.

"Janet." He awkwardly rose from his chair and crouched, not so much in courtesy as to relieve the pressure on his heart.

"Whatever brings you back to these parts?" She was taking the pose that she was just anyone who once knew him.

He slumped back. "I'm always coming back. It's just you've never been here."

"Well, I've"—she seated herself on an orange bench and crossed her plump legs cockily—"been in Germany with my husband."

"He was in the Air Force."

"Yes." It startled her a little that he knew.

"And he's out now?" Clyde had never met him, but having now seen Janet again, he felt he knew him well—a slight, literal fellow, to judge from the shallowness of the marks he had left on her. He would wear eyebrow-style glasses, be a griper, have some not quite negotiable talent, like playing the clarinet or drawing political cartoons, and now be starting up a drab avenue of business. Selling insurance, most likely. Poor Janet, Clyde felt; except for the interval of himself— his splendid, perishable self—she would never see the light. Yet she had retained her beautiful calm, a sleepless tranquility marked by that pretty little blue puffiness below the eyes. And either she had grown slimmer or he had grown more tolerant of fat. Her thick ankles and the general *obstinacy* of her flesh used to goad him into being cruel.

"Yes." Her voice indicated that she had withdrawn; perhaps some ugliness of their last parting had recurred to her.

"I was 4-F." He was ashamed of this, and his confessing

it, though she seemed unaware of the change, turned their talk inward. "A peacetime slacker," he went on, "what could be more ignoble?"

She was quiet a while, then asked, "How many children do you have?"

"Two. Age three and one. A girl and a boy; very symmetrical. Do you"—he blushed lightly, and brushed at his forehead to hide it—"have any?"

"No, we thought it wouldn't be fair, until we were more fixed."

Now the quiet moment was his to hold; she had matched him failing for failing. She recrossed her legs, and in a quaint strained way smiled.

"I'm trying to remember," he admitted, "the last time we saw each other. I can't remember how we broke up."

"I can't either," she said. "It happened so often."

Clyde wondered if with that sarcasm she intended to fetch his eyes to the brink of tears of grief. Probably not; premeditation had never been much of a weapon for her, though she had tried to learn it from him.

He moved across the linoleum to sit on the bench beside her. "I can't tell you," he said, "how much, of all the people in this town, you were the one I wanted to see." It was foolish, but he had prepared it to say, in case he ever saw her again.

"Why?" This was more like her: blunt, pucker-lipped curiosity. He had forgotten it.

"Well, hell. Any number of reasons. I wanted to say something."

"What?"

"Well, that if I hurt you, it was stupidity, because I was young. I've often wondered since if I did, because it seems now that you were the only person outside my family who ever, actually, *liked* me."

"Did I?"

"If you think by doing nothing but asking monosyllabic questions you're making an effect, you're wrong."

She averted her face, leaving, in a sense, only her body— the pale, columnar breadth of arm, the freckled crescent of shoulder muscle under the cotton strap of her summer dress —with him. "You're the one who's making effects." It was such a wan, senseless thing to say to defend herself; Clyde, virtually paralyzed by so heavy an injection of love, touched her arm icily.

With a quickness that suggested she had foreseen this, she got up and went to the table by the bay window, where rows of overlapping magazines were laid. She bowed her head to their titles, the nape of her neck in shadow beneath a half-collapsed bun. She had always had trouble keeping her hair pinned.

Clyde was blushing intensely. "Is your husband working around here?"

"He's looking for work." That she kept her back turned while saying this gave him hope.

"Mr. Behn?" The petite secretary-nurse, switching like a pendulum, led him back through the sanctums and motioned for him to sit in a high hinged chair padded with black leather. Pennypacker's equipment had always made him nervous; tons of it were marshalled through the rooms. A complex tree of tubes and lenses leaned over his left shoulder, and by his right elbow a porcelain basin was cupped expectantly. An eye chart crisply stated gibberish. In time Pennypacker himself appeared: a tall, stooped man with mottled cheekbones and an air of suppressed anger.

"Now what's the trouble, Clyde?"

"It's nothing; I mean it's very little," Clyde began, laughing inappropriately. During his adolescence he had developed a joking familiarity with his dentist and his regular doctor, but he had never become intimate with Pennypacker, who remained, what he had seemed at first, an aloof administrator of expensive humiliations. In the third grade he had made Clyde wear glasses. Later, he annually cleaned, with a shrill push of hot water, wax from Clyde's ears, and once had thrust two copper straws up Clyde's nostrils in a futile attempt to purge his sinuses. Clyde always felt unworthy of Pennypacker, felt himself a dirty conduit balking the smooth onward flow of the doctor's reputation and apparatus. He blushed to mention his latest trivial stoppage. "It's just that for over two months I've had this eyelid that twitters and it makes it difficult to think."

Pennypacker drew little circles with a pencil-sized flashlight in front of Clyde's right eye.

"It's the left lid," Clyde said, without daring to turn his head. "I went to a doctor up where I live, and he said it was like a rattle in the fender and there was nothing to do. He said it would go away, but it didn't and didn't, so I had my mother make an appointment for when I came down here to visit."

Pennypacker moved to the left eye and drew even closer. The distance between the doctor's eyes and the corners of his mouth was very long; the emotional impression of his face close up was like that of those first photographs taken from rockets, in which the earth's curvature was made apparent. "How do you like being in your home territory?" Pennypacker asked.

"Fine."

"Seem a little strange to you?"

The question itself seemed strange. "A little."

"Mm. That's interesting."

"About the eye, there were two things I thought. One was, I got some glasses made in Massachusetts by a man nobody else ever went to, and I thought his prescription might be faulty. His equipment seemed so ancient and kind of full of cobwebs; like a Dürer print." He never could decide how cultured Pennypacker was; the Canadian lake argued against it, but he was county-famous in his trade, in a county where doctors were as high as the intellectual scale went.

The flashlight, a tepid sun girdled by a grid of optical circles behind which Pennypacker's face loomed dim and colorless, came right to the skin of Clyde's eye, and the vague face lurched forward angrily, and Clyde, blind in a world of light, feared that Pennypacker was inspecting the floor of his soul. Paralyzed by panic, he breathed, "The other was that something might be in it. At night it feels as if there's a tiny speck deep in under the lid."

Pennypacker reared back and insolently raked the light back and forth across Clyde's face. "How long have you had this flaky stuff on your lids?"

The insult startled Clyde. "Is there any?"

"How long have you had it?"

"Some mornings I notice little grains like salt that I thought were what I used to call sleepy-dust—"

"This isn't sleepy-dust," the doctor said. He repeated, "This isn't sleepy-dust." Clyde started to smile at what he took to be kidding of his childish vocabulary, but Pennypacker cut him short with "Cases of this can lead to loss of the eye-lashes."

"Really?" Clyde was vain of his lashes, which in his boyhood had been exceptionally long, giving his face the alert and tender look of a girl's. "Do you think it's the reason for the tic?" He imagined his face with the lids bald and the lashes lying scattered on his cheeks like insect legs. "What can I do?"

"Are you using your eyes a great deal?"

"Some. No more than I ever did."

Pennypacker's hands, blue after Clyde's dazzlement, lifted an intense brown bottle from a drawer. "It may be bacteria, it may be allergy; when you leave I'll give you something that should knock it out either way. Do you follow me? Now, Clyde"—his voice became murmurous and consolatory as he placed a cupped hand, rigid as an electrode, on the top of Clyde's head—"I'm going to put some drops in your eyes so we can check the prescription of the glasses you bought in Massachusetts."

Clyde didn't remember that the drops stung so; he gasped outright and wept while Pennypacker held the lids apart with his finger and worked them gently open and shut, as if he were playing with snapdragons. Pennypacker set preposterously small, circular dark brown glasses on Clyde's face and in exchange took away the stylish horn-rims Clyde had kept in his pocket. It was Pennypacker's method to fill his little rooms with waiting patients and wander from one to another like a dungeon-keeper.

Clyde heard, far off, the secretary's voice tinkle, and, amplified by the hollow hall, Pennypacker's rumble in welcome and Janet's respond. The one word "headaches," petulantly emphasized, stood up in her answer. Then a door was shut. Silence.

Clyde admired how matter-of-fact she had sounded. He had always admired this competence in her, her authority in the world peripheral to the world of love in which she was so servile. He remembered how she could outface waitresses and how she would bluff her mother when this vicious woman unexpectedly entered the screened porch where they were supposed to be playing cribbage. Potted elephant plants sat in the corners of the porch like faithful dwarfs; robins had built a nest in the lilac outside, inches from the screen. It had been taken as an omen, a blessing, when one evening their being on the glider no longer distressed the birds.

Unlike, say, the effects of Novocain, the dilation of pupils is impalpable. The wallpaper he saw through the open door seemed as distinct as ever. He held his fingernails close to his nose and was unable to distinguish the cuticles. He touched the sides of his nose, where tears had left trails. He looked at his fingers again, and they seemed fuzzier. He couldn't see his fingerprint whorls. The threads of his shirt had melted into an elusive liquid surface.

A door opened and closed, and another patient was ushered into a consulting room and imprisoned by Pennypacker. Janet's footsteps had not mingled with the others. Without ever quite sacrificing his reputation for good behavior, Clyde in high school had become fairly bold in heckling teachers he considered stupid or unjust. He got out of his chair, looked down the hall to where a white splinter of secretary showed, and quickly walked past a closed door to one ajar. His blood told him, This one.

Janet was sitting in a chair as upright as the one he had left, a two-pronged comb in her mouth, her back arched and her arms up, bundling her hair. As he slipped around the door, she plucked the comb from between her teeth and laughed at him. He saw in a little rimless mirror cocked above her head his own head, grimacing with stealth and grotesquely costumed in glasses like two chocolate coins, and appreciated her laughter, though it didn't fit with what he had prepared to say. He said it anyway: "Janet, are you happy?"

She rose with a practical face and walked past him and clicked the door shut. As she stood facing it, listening for a reaction from outside, he gathered her hair in his hand and lifted it from the nape of her neck, which he had expected to find in shadow but which was instead, to his distended eyes, bright as a candle. He clumsily put his lips to it.

"Don't you love your wife?" she asked.

"Incredibly much," he murmured into the fine neck-down.

She moved off, leaving him leaning awkwardly, and in front of the mirror smoothed her hair away from her ears. She sat down again, crossing her wrists in her lap.

"I just got told my eyelashes are going to fall out," Clyde said.

"Your pretty lashes," she said sombrely.

"Why do you hate me?"

"Shh. I don't hate you now."

"But you did once."

"No, I did *not* once. Clyde what *is* this bother? What are you after?"

"Son of a bitch, so I'm a bother. I knew it. You've just forgotten, all the time I've been remembering; you're so *damn* dense. I come in here a bundle of pain to tell you I'm sorry and I want you to be happy, and all I get is the back of your neck." Affected by what had happened to his eyes, his tongue had loosened, pouring out impressions; with culminating incoherence he dropped to his knees beside her chair, wondering if the thump would bring Pennypacker. "I must see you again," he blurted.

"Shh."

"I come back here and the only person who was ever pleasant to me I discover I maltreated so much she hates me."

"Clyde," she said, "you didn't maltreat me. You were a good boy to me."

Straightening up on his knees, he fumbled his fingers around the hem of the neck of her dress and pulled it out and looked down into the blurred cavity between her breasts. He had a remembrance of her freckles going down from her shoulders into her bathing suit. His glasses hit her cheek.

She stabbed the back of his hand with the points of her comb and he got to his feet, rearing high into a new, less sorrowful atmosphere. "When?" he asked, short of breath.

"No," she said.

"What's your married name?"

"Clyde, I thought you were successful. I thought you had beautiful children. Aren't you happy?"

"I am, I am; but"—the rest was so purely inspired its utterance only grazed his lips—"happiness isn't everything."

Footsteps ticked down the hall, toward their door, past it. Fear emptied his chest, yet with an excellent imitation of his old high-school flippancy he blew her a kiss, waited, opened the door, and whirled through it. His hand had left the knob when the secretary, emerging from the room where he should have been, confronted him in the linoleum-smelling hall. "Where could I get a drink of water?" he asked plaintively, assuming the hunch and whine of a blind beggar. In truth, he had, without knowing it, become thirsty.

"Once a year I pass through your territory," Pennypacker intoned as he slipped a growing weight of lenses into the tin frame on Clyde's nose. He had returned to Clyde more relaxed and chatty, now that all his little rooms were full. Clyde had tried to figure out from the pattern of noise, if Janet had been dismissed. He believed she had. The thought made his eyelid throb. He didn't even know her married name. "Down the Turnpike," Pennypacker droned on, while his face flickered in and out of focus, "up the New Jersey Pike, over the George Washington Bridge, up the Merritt, then up Route 7 all the way to Lake Champlain. To hunt the big bass. There's an experience for you."

"I notice you have a new clock in your waiting room."

"That's a Christmas present from the Alton Optical Company. Can you read that line?"

"H, L, F, Y, T, something that's either an S or an E—"

"K," Pennypacker said without looking. The poor devil, he had all those letters memorized, all that gibberish—abruptly, Clyde wanted to love him. The oculist altered one lens. "Is it better this way? . . . Or this way?"

At the end of the examination, Pennypacker said, "Though the man's equipment was dusty, he gave you a good prescription. In your right eye the axis of astigmatism has rotated several degrees, which is corrected in the lenses. If you have been experiencing a sense of strain, part of the reason, Clyde, is that these heavy frames are slipping down on your nose and giving you a prismatic effect. For a firm fit you should have metal frames, with adjustable nose pads."

"They leave such ugly dents on the sides of your nose."

"You should have them. Your bridge, you see"—he tapped his own—"is recessed. It takes a regular face to support unarticulated frames. Do you wear your glasses all the time?"

"For the movies and reading. When I got them in the third grade you told me that was all I needed them for."

"You should wear them all the time."

"Really? Even just for walking around?"

"All the time, yes. You have middle-aged eyes."

Pennypacker gave him a little plastic squeeze bottle of drops. "That is for the fungus on your lids."

"Fungus? There's a brutal thought. Well, will it cure the tic?"

Pennypacker impatiently snapped, "The tic is caused by muscular fatigue."

Thus Clyde was dismissed into a tainted world where things evaded his focus. He went down the hall in his sunglasses and was told by the secretary that he would receive a bill. The waiting room was full now, mostly with downcast old men and myopic children gnawing at their mothers. From out of this crowd a ripe young woman arose and came against his chest, and Clyde, included in the intimacy of the aroma her hair and skin gave off, felt weak and broad and grand, like a declining rose. Janet tucked a folded note into the pocket of his shirt and said conversationally, "He's waiting outside in the car."

The neutral, ominous "he" opened wide a conspiracy Clyde instantly entered. He stayed behind a minute, to give her time to get away. Ringed by the judging eyes of the young and old, he felt like an actor snug behind the blinding protection of the footlights; he squinted prolongedly at the speedometer-clock, which, like a letter delivered on the stage, in fact was blank. Then, smiling ironically toward both sides, he left the waiting room, coming into Pennypacker's entrance hall, a cubicle equipped with a stucco umbrella stand and a red rubber mat saying, in letters so large he could read them, WALK IN.

He had not expected to be unable to read her note. He held it at arm's length and slowly brought it toward his face, wiggling it in the light from outdoors. Though he did this several times, it didn't yield even the simplest word. Just wet blue specks. Under the specks, however, in their intensity and disposition, he believed he could make out the handwriting —slanted, open, unoriginal—familiar to him from other notes received long ago. This glimpse, through the skin of the paper, of her plain self quickened and sweetened his desire more than touching her had. He tucked the note back into his shirt pocket and its stiffness there made a shield for his heart. In this armor he stepped into the familiar street. The maples, macadam, shadows, houses, cement, were to his violated eyes as brilliant as a scene remembered; he became a child again in this town, where life was a distant adventure, a rumor, an always imminent joy.

Still Life

LEONARD HARTZ, a slender and earnest American with an unromantically round head, came to the Constable School because it was one of three British art schools approved by the Veterans Administration under the new, pruned GI Bill. He could not imagine what the V.A. had seen in the place. Constable—"Connie" to the bird-tongued, red-legged girls who composed half its student body—was at once pedantic and frivolous. The vast university museum which, with a gesture perhaps less motherly than absent-mindedly inclusive, sheltered the school in its left wing was primarily archaeological in interest. Upstairs, room after room was packed with glass cases of Anglo-Saxon rubble; downstairs, a remarkably complete set of casts taken from classical statuary swarmed down corridors and gestured under high archways in a kind of petrified riot. This counterfeit wealth of statues, many of them still decorated with the seams of the casting process and quite swarthy with dust, was only roughly ordered. Beginning in the east with wasp-waisted *kouroi* whose Asiatic faces wore the first faint smile of the Attic dawn, one passed through the jumbled poignance and grandeur of Greece's golden age and ended in a neglected, westerly room where some huge coarse monuments of the Roman-Christian degeneracy rested their hypnotized stares in the shadows. Masterpieces lurked like spies in this mob. His first week, Leonard spent a morning and two afternoons sketching a blackened Amazon leaning half-clad from a dark corner, and only at the end of the second day, struck by a resemblance between his sketch and the trademark of an American pencil manufacturer, did he realize that his silent companion had been the Venus de Milo.

For freshmen at the Constable School were to start off banished from the school itself, with its bright chatter and gay smocks, and sent into these sad galleries to "draw from

27

the antique." The newcomers—Leonard and four other re-
sentful American veterans and one wispy English boy and
a dozen sturdy English teen-age girls—straggled each morning into the museum, gripping a drawing-board under one arm
and a bench called a "horse" under the other, and at dusk,
which came early to the interior of the museum, returned
with their burdens, increased by the weight of a deity pinned
to their boards, in time to see the advanced students jostle
at the brush-cleaning sink and the model, incongruously
dressed in street clothes, emerge from her closet. The school
always smelled of turpentine at this hour.

Its disconsolate scent lingering in his head, Leonard left
the school alone, hurrying down the three ranks of shallow
steps just in time to miss his bus. Everywhere he turned, those
first weeks, he had this sensation of things evading him. When
he did board his bus, and climbed to the second deck, the
store fronts below sped backwards as if from pursuit—the
chemist's shops that were not exactly drugstores, the tea
parlors that were by no means luncheonettes. The walls of
the college buildings, crusty and impregnable, swept past
like an armada of great gray sails, and the little river sung by
Drayton and Milton and Matthew Arnold slipped from under
him, and at right angles to the curving road red suburban
streets plunged down steep perspectives, bristling with hedges
and spiked walls and knotted chains. Sometimes, suspended
between the retreating brick rows like puffs of flak, a flock
of six or so birds was turning and flying, invariably away.
The melancholy of the late English afternoon was seldom
qualified for Leonard by any expectation of the night. Of the
four other Americans, three were married, and although
each of these couples in turn had him over for supper and
Scrabble, these meals quickly vanished in his evenings' recur-
rent, thankless appetite. The American movies so readily
available reaffirmed rather than relieved his fear that he was
out of contact with anything that might give him strength.
Even at the school, where he had decided to place himself
at least provisionally under the influence of Professor Seabright's musty aesthetic, he began to feel that indeed there
was, in the precise contour of a shoulder and the unique
shape of space framed between Apollo's legs, something intensely important, which, too—though he erased until the
paper tore and squinted till his eyes burned—evaded him.

Seabright tried to visit the students among the casts once
a day. Footsteps would sound briskly, marking the instructor

off from any of the rare sightseers, usually a pair of nuns, who wandered, with whispers and a soft slithering step, into this section of the museum. Seabright's voice, its lisp buried in the general indistinctness, would rumble from far away, as if the gods were thinking of thundering. In stages of five minutes each, it would draw nearer, and eventually spoke distinctly with the student on the other side of the pedestals, a tall English girl named, with a pertness that sat somewhat askew on her mature body, Robin.

"Here, here," Seabright said. "We're not doing silhouettes."

"I thought, you know," Robin replied in an eager voice that to Leonard's American ears sounded also haughty, "if the outline came right, the rest could be fitted in."

"Oh no. Oh no. We don't fit *in;* we build *across* the large form. Otherwise all the little pieces will never read. You see, there, we don't even know where the center of your chest is. Ah—may I?" From the grunts and sighs Leonard pictured Robin rising from straddling her horse and Seabright seating himself. "Dear me," he said, "you've got the outlines so black they rather take my eye. However . . ."

To Leonard it was one of Seabright's charms that, faced with any problem of drawing, he became so engrossed he forgot to teach. He had had to train himself to keep glancing at his watch; else he would sit the whole afternoon attacking a beginner's exercise, frowning like a cat at a mouse hole, while the forgotten student stood by on aching legs.

"There," Seabright sighed reluctantly. "I'm afraid I've spent my time with you. It's just one passage, but you can see here, across the thorax, how the little elements already are turning the large surface. And then, as you'd pass into the rib cage, with these two shadows just touched in at first, you see . . . Perhaps I should do a *bit* more . . . There, you see. And then we could pass on to the throat. . . . It's a good idea, actually, on these figgers to start with the pit of the throat, and then work the shoulders outward and go up for the head. . . ."

"Yes sir," Robin said, a shade impatiently.

"The whole thrust of the pose is in those angles, you see? Do you see?"

"Yes, sir, I hope so."

But her hopes were not enough for him; he came around the pedestals and his plump, solemn, slightly feline figure was in Leonard's view when he turned and said apprehensively to the hidden girl, "You understand to use the pencil as lightly as you can? Work up the whole form gradually?"

"Oh, yes. Quite," Robin's bright voice insisted.

Seabright twitched his head and came and stood behind Leonard. "I don't think," he said at last, "we need draw in the casting seams; we can idealize to that extent."

"It seemed to help in getting the intervals," Leonard explained.

"Even though these are exercises, you know, there's no advantage in having them, uh, positively ugly." Leonard glanced around at his teacher, who was not usually sarcastic, and Seabright continued with some embarrassment; his speech impediment was less audible than visible, a fitful effortfulness of the lips. "I must confess you're not given much help by your subject matter." His eyes had lifted to the statue Leonard had chosen to draw, for the reason that it had four limbs. Completeness was the crude token by which Leonard preferred one statue to another; he was puzzled by Seabright's offended murmur of "Wretched thing."

"Beg pardon, sir?"

"Look here, Hartz," Seabright exclaimed, and with startling aggressiveness trotted forward, stretched up on tiptoe, and slapped the plaster giant's side. "The Roman who copied this didn't even understand that this side is constricted by this leg taking the weight!" Seabright himself constricted, then blinked abashedly and returned to Leonard's side with a more cautious voice. "Nevertheless, you've carried parts of it with admirable intensity. Per, uh, perhaps you've been rather *too* intense; relax a bit at first and aim for the swing of the figger—how that little curve here, you see, sets up against this long lean one." Leonard expected him to ask for the pencil, but instead he asked, "Why don't you get yourself a new statue? That charming girl Miss Cox is doing—Venus, really, I suppose she is. At least there you do get some echoes of the Greek grace. I should think you've done your duty by this one."

"O.K. It *was* starting to feel like mechanical drawing." To dramatize his obedience, Leonard began prying out his thumbtacks, but Seabright, his five minutes not used up, lingered.

"You do see some sense in drawing these at the outset, don't you?" Seabright was troubled by his American students; of the five, Leonard knew he must seem the least rebellious.

"Sure. It's quite challenging, once you get into one."

The Englishman was not totally reassured. He hovered apologetically, and confided this anecdote: "Picasso, you know, had a woman come to him for advice about learning to draw, and he told her right off, '*Dessinez antiques.*' Draw from the antique. There's nothing like it, for getting the big forms."

Then Seabright left, pattering past threatening athletes and emperors, through the archway, out of the section altogether, into the gayer room where medieval armor, spurs, rings, spoons, and chalices were displayed. The sound of his shoes died. From behind the hedge of pedestals, quite close to Leonard's ear, Robin's clear voice piped, "Well isn't Puss in a snorty mood?"

To attack the statue Seabright assigned him, Leonard moved his horse several yards forward, without abandoning the precious light that filtered through a window high behind him. From this new position Robin was in part visible. A plinth still concealed her bulk, but around the plinth's corner her propped drawing-board showed, and her hand when it stabbed at the paper, and even her whole head, massive with floppy fair hair, when she bent forward into a detail. He was at first too shy to risk meeting her eyes, so her foot, cut off at the ankle and thus isolated in its blue ballet slipper on the shadowy marble floor, received the brunt of his attention. It was a long foot, with the division of the toes just beginning at the rim of the slipper's blue arc, and the smooth pallor of the exposed oval yielding, above the instep, to the mist-reddened roughness of the Englishwoman's leg. These national legs, thick at the ankles and glazed up to the knees with a kind of weatherproofing, on Robin were not homely; like a piece of fine pink ceramic her ankle kept taking, in Seabright's phrase, his eye.

After an hour he brought out, "Aren't your feet cold, in just those slippers?"

"Rather," she promptly responded and, with the quick skip that proved to be her custom, went beyond the question: "Gives me the shivers all over, being in this rotten place."

It was too quick for him. "You mean the school?"

"Oh, the school's all right; it's these wretched antiques."

"Don't you like them? Don't you find them sort of stable, and timeless?"

"If these old things are timeless, I'd rather be timely by a long shot."

"No, seriously. Think of them as angels."

"Seriously my foot. You Americans are never serious. Everything you say's a variety of joke; honestly, it's like conversing in a monkey-house."

On this severe note Leonard feared they had concluded; but a minute later she showed him his silence was too careful by lucidly announcing, "I have a friend who's an atheist and hopes World War Three blows everything to bits. He doesn't care. He's an atheist."

Their subsequent conversations sustained this discouraging quality, of two creatures thrown together in the same language exchanging, across a distance wider than it seemed, miscalculated signals. He felt she quite misjudged his earnestness and would have been astonished to learn how deeply and solidly she had been placed in his heart, affording a fulcrum by which he lifted the great dead mass of his spare time, which now seemed almost lighter than air, a haze of quixotic expectations, imagined murmurs, easy undressings, and tourist delights. He believed he was coming to love England. He went to a tailor and bought for four guineas a typical jacket of stiff green wool, only to discover, before the smeary mirror in his digs, that it made his head look absurdly small, like one berry on top of a bush; and he kept wearing his little zippered khaki windbreaker to the Constable School.

On his side, he could not estimate how silly she truly was. She was eighteen, and described looking up as a child and seeing bombs floatingly fall from the belly of a German bomber, yet there was something flat and smooth behind her large eyes that deflected his words oddly; she seemed to be empty of the ragged, absorbent wisdom of girls at home whose war experiences stopped short at scrap drives. Across Robin's incongruities—between her name and body, her experiences and innocence—was braced a certain official austerity, a determined erectness of carriage, as if she were Britannia in the cartoons, and her contours contained nothing erotic but limned a necessarily female symbol of ancient militance. Robin was tall, and her figure, crossing back and forth through the shadows of the casts and the patchy light between, seemed to Leonard to stalk. She was always in and out now. In at nine-thirty, breathless; out at ten for a coffee break; back at eleven; lunch at eleven-thirty; back by one; at two-thirty, out for a smoke; in by three; gone by four. Since the days of their joint attack on the Esquiline Venus, her work habits had grown blithe. She had moved away to another area, to analyze

another figure, and he had not been bold enough to follow
with his horse, though his next statue took him in her direction. So at least once an hour she came into his eyes, and,
though the coffee breaks and long lunches forced him to
deduce a lively alien society, he, accustomed by the dragged-
out days of army life to patience, still thought of her as partly
his. It seemed natural, when, three weeks before the Michaelmas term ended, the Puss—Leonard had fallen in with
mocking Seabright—promoted them to still life together.

At the greengrocer's on Monday morning they purchased
still-life ingredients. The Constable School owned a great bin
of inanimate objects, from which Leonard had selected an
old mortar and pestle. His idea was then to buy, to make a
logical picture, some vegetables that could be ground, and to
arrange them in a Chardinesque tumble. But what, really, was
ground, except nuts? The grocer did have some Jamaican
walnuts.

"Don't be funny, Leonard," Robin said. "All those horrid
little wrinkles, we'd be at it forever."

"Well, what else could you grind?"

"We're not going to *grind* anything; we're going to paint
it. What we want is something *smooth*."

"Oranges, miss?" the lad in charge offered.

"Oh, oranges. Everyone's doing oranges—looks like a pack
of advertisements. What we want . . ." Frowning, she surveyed the produce, and Leonard's heart, plunged in the novel
intimacy of shopping with a woman, beat excitedly. "Onions,"
Robin declared. "Onions are what we want."

"Onions, miss?"

"Yes, three, and a cabbage."

"One cabbage?"

"Here, may I pick it out?"

"But, Robin," Leonard said, having never before called her
by name, "onions and cabbages don't go together."

"Really, Leonard, you keep talking as if we're going to *eat*
them."

"They're both so round."

"I dare say. You won't get me doing any globby squashes.
Besides, Leonard, ours won't get rotten."

"Our globby squashes?"

"Our *still* life, sweet. Haven't you seen Melissa's pears?
Really, if I had to look at those brown spots all day I think
I'd go sick."

The lad, in his gray apron and muddy boots, gently pushed a paper bag against her arm. "Tenpence, miss. Five for the onions and four for the head and the bag's a penny."

"Here," Leonard said hoarsely, and the action of handing over the money was so husbandly he blushed.

Robin asked, "Are the onions attractive?"

"Oh yes," the boy said in a level uncomprehending tone that defended him against any meaning she might have, including that of "having him on."

"Did you give us attractive onions?" she repeated. "I mean, we're not going to eat them."

"Oh yes. They're good-looking, miss."

The boy's referring to the cabbage simply as "the head" haunted Leonard, and he started as if at a ghost when, emerging with Robin into the narrow street, the head of a passer-by looked vividly familiar; it was the head alone, for otherwise Jack Fredericks had quite blended in. He was dressed completely in leather and wool, and even the haircut framing his amazed gape of recognition had the heavy British form. Eerie reunions are common among Americans in Europe, but Leonard had never before been hailed from this far in the past. It offended him to have his privacy, built during so many painful weeks of loneliness, unceremoniously crashed; yet he was pleased to be discovered with a companion so handsome. "Jack, this is Miss Robin Cox; Robin, Jack Fredericks. Jack is from my home town, Wheeling."

"Wheeling, in what state?" the girl asked.

"West Virginia," Jack smiled. "It's rather like your Black Country."

"More green than black," Leonard said.

Jack guffawed. "Good old literal Len," he told Robin. His small moist eyes sought in vain to join hers in a joke over their mutual friend. He and Leonard had never been on a "Len" basis. Had they met on the streets of Wheeling, neither one would have stopped walking.

"What are you doing here?" Leonard asked him.

"Reading Ec at Jesus; but you're the one who baffles me. You're *not* at the university surely?"

"Sort of. We're both at the Constable School of Art. It's affiliated."

"I've never *heard* of it!" Jack laughed out loud, for which Leonard was grateful, since Robin further stiffened.

"It's in a wing of the museum. It's a very pleasant place."

"Is it *really*? Well I must come over sometime and see this strange institution. I'm rather interested in painting right now."

"Sure. Come on over. Anytime. We have to get back now and make a still life out of these onions."

"Well, aren't you *won*derful? You know," Jack said to the girl, "Len was a year older than I in public school and I'm used to looking up at him."

To this preposterous lie Robin coolly replied with another: "Oh at Connie we all look up to him."

The Constable School could not afford to waste its precious space on still lifes, and imposed upon the museum's good nature by setting them up in the Well, a kind of basement with a skylight. Here hard-to-classify casts were stashed. Here a great naturalistic boar reclined on his narrow tufted bottom; the Dying Gaul sunned himself in the soft light sifting from above like dust; Winged Victory hoisted her battered feathers; and a tall hermaphrodite, mutilated by Byzantine piety, posed behind a row of brutal Roman portrait busts. The walls were a strange gay blue; even more strangely gay were the five or six students, foreshortened into chipper, quick shapes, chirping around tables of brilliant fruit. As he followed his friend's blond hair down the reverberating iron of the spiral stairs, Leonard felt he had at last arrived at the radiant heart of the school.

Nowhere in the museum was there as much light as in the Well. Their intimacy of the grocer's shop seemed clarified and enhanced in the fall of light, and pointed by artistic purpose. With much minuteness they arranged the elements upon a yellow cloth. Her white hands fussed imperiously with the cabbage, tearing off leaf after leaf until she had reduced it to a roundness she imagined would be simple to draw. After lunch they began to mark with charcoal their newly bought canvases, which smelled of glue and green wood. To have her, some distance from his side, echoing his task, and to know that her eyes concentrated into the same set of shapes, which after a little concentration took on an unnatural intensity, like fruit in Paradise, curiously enlarged his sense of his physical size; he seemed to tower above the flagstones, and his voice, in responding to her erratic exclamations and complaints, struck into his ears with grave finality, as if his words were being incised into the air. The other students on still life also worked solemnly, and in the after-

noon there were few of them. The sounds of museum traffic
drifted in from a comparatively dark and cluttered world.

Jack Fredericks paid his visit the very next day. He
thumped down the stairs in his little scholar's gown and stared
at the still life over Robin's shoulder and asked, "Why are
you going to grind onions in a mortar?"

"We're not," she replied in the haughty voice Leonard had
first heard.

Jack sauntered over to the hermaphrodite and said "Good
Lord. What happened to *him?*"

Leonard made no earnest effort to put him at his ease.
Embarrassed and hence stubborn, Jack lay down on the
shallow ledge designed to set off the exhibits, in a place just
behind the table supporting the still life, and smiled up
quizzically at the faces of the painters. He meant to look
debonair, but in the lambent atmosphere he looked ponderous,
with all that leather and wool. The impression of mass was
so intense Leonard feared he might move and break one of
the casts. Leonard had not noticed on the street how big his
fellow West Virginian had grown. The weight was mostly
in flesh: broad beefy hands folded on his vest, corpulent
legs uneasily crossed on the cold stone floor.

Seabright made no pretense of not being startled at finding
him there. "What uh, what are you doing?"

"I guess I'm auditing."

The telltale "guess" put the Puss's back up higher. "We
don't generally set aside space for spectators."

"Oh, I've been very unobtrusive, sir. We haven't been
saying a word to each other."

"Be that as it may, you're right in these people's vision.
If you didn't come down here to look at the statues, I'm
really afraid there's nothing here for you."

"Oh. Well. Certainly." Jack, grimacing with the effort,
raised his body to his feet. "I didn't know there were regula-
tions."

Leonard did not strenuously follow up this victory. His
courtship of Robin continued as subtly as before, though
twice he did dare ask her to the movies. The second time, she
accepted. The delicately tinted Japanese love tale, so queerly
stained with murders, seemed to offer a mutually foreign
ground where they might meet as equals, but the strict rules
of the girls' house where she stayed, requiring them to scamper
directly into a jammed bus, made the whole outing in the
end, seem awkward and foolish. He much preferred the

days, full of light and time, when their proximity had the grace of the accidental and before their eyes a constant topic of intercourse was poised. He even wondered if through their one date he hadn't lost some dignity in her eyes. The tone of her talk to him in the Well was respectful; the more so since his painting was coming excellently. Something in those spherical shapes and mild colors spoke to him. Seabright was plainly flattered by his progress. "Mmm," he would purr, "delicious tones on the shadow side here. But I believe you're shading a bit too much toward red. It's really a very distinct violet, you know. If I could have your palette a moment. . . . And a clean brush?" Lesson by lesson, Leonard was drawn into Seabright's world, a tender, subdued world founded on violet, and where violet—pronounced "vaalet"—at the faintest touch of a shadow, at the slightest hesitation of red or blue, rose to the surface, shyly vibrant. Robin's bluntly polychrome vision caused him to complain, "Really, Miss Cox, I wish you had got the drawing correct before you began filling in the spaces." When Puss had gone back up the spiral stair, Robin would transfer his complaint to Leonard as "Honestly, Len, I can't see all this rotten purple. You'd think my onions were grapes, to see what he's done to them. Tell me, should I scrape his paint right off?"

Leonard walked around to her easel and suggested, "Why don't you try keying in the rest of it around them?"

"Key it in? Key it in!" She seemed to relish the shrill syllables.

"Sure. Make your cabbage kind of greeny-purple, and the yellow cloth browny-purple, and for the mortar, well, try pure turps."

"No," she pouted. "It's not a joke. You're just being a disgusting silly American. You think I'm stupid at paints."

Each day he sank deeper into a fatherly role; he welcomed any secure relationship with her, yet wondered if he wasn't being, perhaps, neutralized. She never sought his advice except on technical matters until the day near the end of term when, conceding him in this sense a great stride forward, she asked, "How well do you know your friend Jack Fredericks?"

"Not well at all. I wouldn't call him my friend. He was a year younger in high school, and we weren't really in the same social class either."

"The social classes in America—are they very strong?"

"Well—the divisions aren't as great as here, but there're more of them."

"And he comes from a good class?"

"Fair." He thought reticence was his best tactic, but when she joined him in silence he was compelled to prod. "What makes you ask?"

"Now, Leonard. You mustn't breathe a word; if you do, I'll absolutely shrivel. You see, he's asked me to model for him."

"*Mode*l for him? He can't paint."

"Yes he can. He's shown me some of his things and they're rather good."

"How does he mean 'model'? Model in what condition?"

"Yes. In the nude." High color burned evenly in her face; she dabbed at the canvas.

"That's ridiculous. He doesn't paint at all."

"But he *does*, Leonard. He's taken it up very seriously. I've *seen* his things."

"What do they look like?"

"Oh, rather abstract."

"I bet."

"*All* you Americans paint in the abstract."

"I don't." He didn't feel this was much of a point to score.

"He says I have a lovely body—"

"Well *I* could have told you *that*." But he hadn't.

"—and *swears*, absolutely, there would be nothing to it. He's even ┄┄┄ d a model's fee."

"Well I never heard of such an embarrassing awful scheme."

"Really, Leonard, it's embarrassing only when you talk of it. I *know* he's perfectly serious as a painter."

Leonard added a fleck of black to a mixture on his palette and sighed. "Well, Robin. You do whatever you want. It's your life."

"Oh, I wouldn't *dream* of *do*ing it. Mummy and Daddy would *die*."

His relief was overwhelmed by a sudden fierce sense of being wronged. "Don't let *them* stand in your way. Why, this may be the start of a whole career for you."

"I mean, I never con*sid*ered it. I was just interested in your opinion of the man."

"My opinion is, he's a *horrible* man. He's a silly spoiled snob and about to get hog fat and I don't see what attracts you in him. Terrible person. Terrible."

"Well, as you say, you don't know him very well."

Leonard and the other unmarried veteran went to Europe during the Michaelmas vacation. On the Channel boat, his thoughts, free for the first time from the tangle of departure, returned to Robin, and the certainty of her turning Fredericks down warmed him on the cold, briny deck. In Paris the idea that she even toyed with such a proposition excited him; it suggested an area of willingness, of loneliness, that Leonard could feasibly invade. In Frankfurt he wondered if actually she would turn him down—he knew she was staying around the university during vacation—and by Hamburg he was certain that she had not; she had consented. He grew accustomed to this conviction as he and his companion slowly circled back through the Lowlands. By the time he disembarked at Dover he was quite indifferent to her nakedness.

The school had grown chillier and much older in four weeks. In the Well, the arrangements of fruit had decayed; with the hope that some of the students would continue to work despite the vacation, the things had not been disturbed. Their own still life was least affected by time. The onions were as immutable as the statues; but the cabbage, peeled by Robin to its solid pale heart, had relaxed in wilting, and its outer leaves, gray and almost transparent, rested on the gold cloth. His painting, still standing in its easel, preserved the original appearance of the cabbage, but the pigments had dulled, sinking into the canvas; their hardness made the painting seem finished, though there were several uncovered corners and numerous contrasts his fresh eye saw the need of adjusting. He loaded his palette and touched paint to the canvas reluctantly. The Well was so empty on this Monday morning of resumption, he felt he had made a mistake, by misreading the schedule, or taking it too seriously. At the far end, the little English boy, who was arrogant as well as wispy, noisily dismantled groups, crashing vegetable elements into a paper sack.

After eleven o'clock, Robin appeared on the balcony of the spiral stair. She overlooked the Well with her serene Britannia stance—her bosom a brave chest, her hips and legs a firm foundation—and then descended in a flurry. "Leonard. Where have you *been?*"

"I told you, I was going to Europe with Max. We went as far east as Hamburg, and came back through Holland and Belgium."

"You went to *Germany?* Whatever for?"

"Well, I am German, eventually."

Her attention went sideways. "I say, the cabbage has taken it hard, hasn't it?" She took her own painting off the easel. "Are you still going at it? Puss has put me back in antique."

"Of all the *crust*."

"Oh, well. He said to me, 'You're pretty rotten at this, aren't you?' and I agreed. It's the truth."

Leonard resented the implication in this blitheness that he, too, the companion of her futile labors, was negligible. His mouth stiff with injury, he sarcastically asked, "How's your posing for Fredericks coming?"

Her blue eyes squared. "Posing for *him?* I did nothing of the sort." Her words might have been "I love you"; his heart felt a sudden draft and he started to say, "I'm glad."

But she went on with surprising intensity, "Really, Leonard, you refuse to take me *seriously*. I could see all along he was a dreadful bore." Her arm held her canvas captive against her side and with her free hand she impatiently pushed floppy hair back from her forehead—a rigid, aristocratic gesture that swept his stir of hope quite away. He had been stupid. He had been stupid to think that if Fredericks were eliminated, that left him. Over here, they were two of a kind, and by his own admission he was Frederick's inferior. She was done with the silly strange lot. After all, boy friends are a serious bit.

Like those flocks of birds seen from the bus window, she had exploded as he watched. Even before she took a backward step, her receding from him seemed so swift he raised his voice in claiming, less in apology than as a fresh basis, "All Americans are bores."

Flight

AT THE AGE OF SEVENTEEN I was poorly dressed and funny-looking, and went around thinking about myself in the third person. "Allen Dow strode down the street and home." "Allen Dow smiled a thin sardonic smile." Consciousness of a special destiny made me both arrogant and shy. Years before, when I was eleven or twelve, just on the brink of ceasing to be a little boy, my mother and I, ᵉe Sunday afternoon—my father was busy, or asleep—hiked up to the top of Shale Hill, a child's mountain that formed one side of the valley that held our town. There the town lay under us, Olinger, perhaps a thousand homes, the best and biggest of them climbing Shale Hill toward us, and beyond them the blocks of brick houses, one- and two-family, the homes of my friends, sloping down to the pale thread of the Alton Pike, which strung together the high school, the tennis courts, the movie theatre, the town's few stores and gasoline stations, the elementary school, the Lutheran church. On the other side lay more homes, including our own, a tiny white patch placed just where the land began to rise toward the opposite mountain, Cedar Top. There were rims and rims of hills beyond Cedar Top, and looking south we could see the pike dissolving in other towns and turning out of sight amid the patches of green and brown farmland, and it seemed the entire county was lying exposed under a thin veil of haze. I was old enough to feel embarrassment at standing there alone with my mother, beside a wind-stunted spruce tree, on a long spine of shale. Suddenly she dug her fingers into the hair on my head and announced, "There we all are, and there we'll all be forever." She hesitated before the word "forever," and hesitated again before adding, "Except you, Allen. You're going to fly." A few birds were hung far out over the valley, at the level of our eyes, and

41

in her impulsive way she had just plucked the image from them, but it felt like the clue I had been waiting all my childhood for. My most secret self had been made to respond, and I was intensely embarrassed, and irritably ducked my head out from under her melodramatic hand.

She was impulsive and romantic and inconsistent. I was never able to develop this spurt of reassurance into a steady theme between us. That she continued to treat me like an ordinary child seemed a betrayal of the vision she had made me share. I was captive to a hope she had tossed off and forgotten. My shy attempts to justify irregularities in my conduct—reading late at night or not coming back from school on time—by appealing to the image of flight were received with a startled blank look, as if I were talking nonsense. It seemed outrageously unjust. Yes, but, I wanted to say, yes, but it's *your* nonsense. And of course it was just this that made my appeal ineffective: her knowing that I had not made it mine, that I cynically intended to exploit both the privileges of being extraordinary and the pleasures of being ordinary. She feared my wish to be ordinary; once she did respond to my protest that I was learning to fly, by crying with red-faced ferocity, "You'll never learn, you'll stick and die in the dirt just like I'm doing. Why should you be better than your mother?"

She had been born ten miles to the south, on a farm she and her mother had loved. Her mother, a small fierce woman who looked more like an Arab than a German, worked in the fields with the men, and drove the wagon to market ten miles away every Friday. When still a tiny girl, my mother rode with her, and my impression of those rides is of fear— the little girl's fear of the gross and beery men who grabbed and hugged her, her fear of the wagon breaking, of the produce not selling, fear of her mother's possible humiliation and of her father's condition when at nightfall they returned. Friday was his holiday, and he drank. His drinking is impossible for me to picture; for I never knew him except as an enduring, didactic, almost Biblical old man, whose one passion was reading the newspapers and whose one hatred was of the Republican Party. There was something public about him; now that he is dead I keep seeing bits of him attached to famous politicians—his watch chain and his plump square stomach in old films of Theodore Roosevelt, his high-top shoes and the tilt of his head in a photograph of Alfalfa Bill Murry. Alfalfa Bill is turning his head to talk, and holds his hat by the crown, pinching it between two fingers and a thumb, a gentle and courtly grip that reminded me so keenly of my grandfather that I tore the picture out of *Life* and put it in a drawer.

Laboring in the soil had never been congenial to my grandfather, though with his wife's help he prospered by it. Then, in an era when success was hard to avoid, he began to invest in stocks. In 1922 he bought our large white home in the town—its fashionable section had not yet shifted to the Shale Hill side of the valley—and settled in to reap his dividends. He believed to his death that women were foolish, and the broken hearts of his two must have seemed specially so. The dignity of finance for the indignity of farming must have struck him as an eminently advantageous exchange. It strikes me that way, too, and how to reconcile my idea of those fear-ridden wagon rides with the grief that my mother insists she and her mother felt at being taken from the farm? Perhaps prolonged fear is a ground of love. Or perhaps, and likelier, the equation is long and complex, and the few factors I know—the middle-aged woman's mannish pride of land, the adolescent girl's pleasure in riding horses across the fields, their common feeling of rejection in Olinger—are enclosed in brackets and heightened by coefficients that I cannot see. Or perhaps it is not love of land but its absence that needs explaining, in my grandfather's fastidiousness and pride. He believed that as a boy he had been abused, and bore his father a grudge that my mother could never understand. Her grandfather to her was a saintly slender giant, over six feet tall when this was a prodigy, who knew the names of everything, like Adam in Eden. In his old age he was blind. When he came out of the house, the dogs rushed forward to lick his hands. When he lay dying, he requested a Gravenstein apple from the tree on the far edge of the meadow, and his son brought him a Krauser from the orchard near the house. The old man refused it, and my grandfather made a second trip, but in my mother's eyes the outrage had been committed, a savage insult insanely without provocation. What had his father done to him? The only specific complaint I ever heard my grandfather make was that when he was a boy and had to fetch water for the men in the fields, his father would tell him sarcastically, "Pick up your feet; they'll come down themselves." How incongruous! As if each generation of parents commits atrocities against their children which by God's decree remain invisible to the rest of the world.

I remember my grandmother as a little dark-eyed woman who talked seldom and who tried to feed me too much, and then as a hook-nosed profile pink against the lemon cushions of the casket. She died when I was seven. All the rest I know about her is that she was the baby of thirteen children, that while she was alive she made our yard one of the most beautiful in town, and that I am supposed to resemble her brother Pete.

My mother was precocious; she was fourteen when they moved, and for three years had been attending the county normal school. She graduated from Lake College, near Philadelphia, when she was only twenty, a tall handsome girl with a deprecatory smile, to judge from one of the curling photographs kept in a shoebox that I was always opening as a child as if it might contain the clue to the quarrels in my house. My mother stands at the end of our brick walk, beside the elaborately trimmed end of our privet hedge—in shape a thick square column mounted by a rough ball of leaf. The ragged arc of a lilac bush in flower cuts into the right edge of the photograph, and behind my mother I can see a vacant lot where there has been a house ever since I can remember. She poses with a kind of country grace in a long fur-trimmed coat, unbuttoned to expose her beads and a short yet somehow demure flapper dress. Her hands are in her coat pockets, a beret sits on one side of her bangs, and there is a swank about her that seemed incongruous to me, examining this picture on the stained carpet of an ill-lit old house in the evening years of the thirties and in the dark of the warring forties. The costume and the girl in it look so up-to-date, so formidable. It was my grandfather's pleasure, in his prosperity, to give her a generous clothes allowance. My father, the penniless younger son of a Presbyterian minister in Passaic, had worked his way through Lake College by waiting on tables, and still speaks with mild resentment of the beautiful clothes that Lillian Baer wore. This aspect of my mother caused me some pain in high school; she was a fabric snob, and insisted on buying my slacks and sports shirts at the best store in Alton, and since we had little money, she bought me few, when of course what I needed was what my classmates had—a wide variety of cheap clothes.

At the time the photograph was taken, my mother wanted

to go to New York. What she would have done there, or exactly what she wanted to do, I don't know; but her father forbade her. "Forbid" is a husk of a word today, but at that time, in that quaint province, in the mouth of an "indulgent father," it apparently was still viable, for the great moist weight of that forbidding continued to be felt in the house for years, and when I was a child, as one of my mother's endless harangues to my grandfather screamed toward its weeping peak, I could feel it around and above me, like a huge root encountered by an earthworm.

Perhaps in a reaction of anger my mother married my father, Victor Dow, who at least took her as far away as Wilmington, where he had made a beginning with an engineering firm. But the depression hit, my father was laid off, and the couple came to the white house in Olinger, where my grandfather sat reading the newspapers that traced his stocks' cautious decline into worthlessness. I was born. My grandmother went around as a cleaning lady, and grew things in our quarter-acre yard to sell. We kept chickens, and there was a large plot of asparagus. After she had died, in a frightened way I used to seek her in the asparagus patch. By midsummer it would be a forest of dainty green trees, some as tall as I was, and in their frothy touch a spirit seemed to speak, and in the soft thick net of their intermingling branches a promise seemed to be caught, as well as a menace. The asparagus trees were frightening; in the center of the patch, far from the house and the alley, I would fall under a spell, and become tiny, and wander among the great smooth green trunks expecting to find a little house with a smoking chimney, and in it my grandmother. She herself had believed in ghosts, which made her own ghost potent. Even now, sitting alone in my own house, a board creaks in the kitchen and I look up fearing she will come through the doorway. And at night, just before I fall asleep, her voice calls my name in a penetrating whisper, or calls, *"Pete."*

My mother went to work in an Alton department store, selling inferior fabric for $14 a week. During the daytime of my first year of life it was my father who took care of me. He has said since, flattering me as he always does, that it was having me on his hands that kept him from going insane. It may have been this that has made my affection for him so inarticulate, as if I were still a wordless infant looking up into the mothering blur of his man's face. And that same shared year helps account, perhaps, for his gentleness with me, for his willingness to praise, as if everything I do has something sad and crippled in it. He feels sorry for me; my birth coincided with the birth of a great misery, a national misery—only recently has he stopped calling me by the nickname "Young America." Around my first birthday he acquired a position teaching arithmetic and algebra in the Olinger high school, and though he was so kind and humorous he couldn't enter a classroom without creating uproarious problems of discipline, he endured it day by day and year by year, and eventually came to occupy a place in this alien town, so that I believe there are now one or two dozen ex-students, men and women nearing middle age, who carry around with them some piece of encouragement my father gave them, or remember some sentence of his that helped shape them. Certainly there are many who remember the antics with which he burlesqued his discomfort in the classroom. He kept a confiscated cap pistol in his desk, and upon getting an especially stupid answer, he would take it out and, wearing a preoccupied, regretful expression, shoot himself in the head.

My grandfather was the last to go to work, and the most degraded by it. He was hired by the borough crew, men who went around the streets shoveling stones and spreading tar. Bulky and ominous in their overalls, wreathed in steam, and associated with dramatic and portentous equipment, these men had grandeur in the eyes of a child, and it puzzled me, as I walked to and from elementary school, that my grandfather refused to wave to me or confess his presence in any way. Curiously strong for a fastidious man, he kept at it well into his seventies, when his sight failed. It was my task then to read his beloved newspapers to him as he sat in his chair by the bay window, twiddling his high-top shoes in the sunshine. I teased him, reading too fast, then maddeningly slow, skipping from column to column to create one long chaotic story; I read him the sports page, which did not interest him, and mumbled the editorials. Only the speed of his feet's twiddling betrayed vexation. When I'd stop, he would plead mildly in his rather beautiful, old-fashioned, elocutionary voice, "Now just the obituaries, Allen. Just the names to see if anyone I know is there." I imagined, as I viciously barked at him the list of names that might contain the name of a friend, that I was avenging my mother; I believed that she hated him, and for her sake I tried to hate him also. From her incessant resurrection of mysterious

attention back home, in competition with the gorgeous Olinger ignorant.

We walked together to the house where the four of us had been boarded, a large white frame owned by an old couple and standing with lonely decency in a semi-slum. Judith and Catharine turned up the walk, but Molly and I, with a diffident decision that I believe came from her initiative, continued, "to walk around the block." We walked miles, stopping off after midnight at a trolley-car-shaped diner. I got a hamburger, and she impressed me by ordering coffee. We walked back to the house and let ourselves in with the key we had been given; but instead of going upstairs to our rooms we sat downstairs in the dark living room and talked softly for more hours.

What did we say? I talked about myself. It is hard to hear, much less remember, what we ourselves say, just as it might be hard for a movie projector, given life, to see the shadows its eye of light is casting. A transcript, could I produce it, of my monologue through the wide turning point of that night, with all its word-by-word conceit, would distort the picture: this living room miles from home, the street light piercing the chinks in the curtains and erecting on the wallpaper rods of light the size of yardsticks, our hosts and companions asleep upstairs, the incessant sigh of my voice, coffee-primed Molly on the floor beside my chair, her stockinged legs stretched out on the rug; and this odd sense in the room, a tasteless and odorless aura unfamiliar to me, as a pool of water widening.

I remember one exchange. I must have been describing the steep waves of fearing death that had come over me ever since early childhood, about one every three years, and I ended by supposing that it would take great courage to be an atheist. "But I bet you'll become one," Molly said. "Just to show yourself that you're brave enough." I felt she overestimated me, and was flattered. Within a few years, while I still remembered many of her words, I realized how touchingly gauche our assumption was that an atheist is a lonely rebel; for mobs of men are united in atheism, and oblivion—the dense lead-like sea that would occasionally sweep over me—is to them a weight as negligible as the faint pressure of their wallets in their hip pockets. This grotesque and tender misestimate of the world flares in my memory of our conversation like one of the innumerable matches we struck.

The room filled with smoke. Too weary to sit, I lay down

on the floor beside her, and stroked her silver arm in silence, yet still was too timid to act on the wide and negative aura that I did not understand was of compliance. On the upstairs landing, as I went to turn into my room, Molly came forward with a prim look and kissed me. With clumsy force I entered the negative space that had been waiting. Her lipstick smeared in little unflattering flecks into the skin around her mouth; it was as if I had been given a face to eat, and the presence of bone—skull under skin, teeth behind lips—impeded me. We stood for a long time under the burning hall light, until my neck began to ache from bowing. My legs were trembling when we finally parted and sneaked into our rooms. In bed I thought, "Allen Dow tossed restlessly," and realized it was the first time that day I had thought of myself in the third person.

On Saturday morning, we lost our debate. I was sleepy and verbose and haughty, and some of the students in the audience began to boo whenever I opened my mouth. The principal came up on the stage and made a scolding speech, which finished me and my cause, untrammeled Germany. On the train back, Catharine and Judith arranged the seating so that they sat behind Molly and me, and spied on only the tops of our heads. For the first time, on that ride home, I felt what it was to bury a humiliation in the body of a woman. Nothing but the friction of my face against hers drowned out the echo of those boos. When we kissed, a red shadow would well under my lids and eclipse the hostile hooting faces of the debate audience, and when our lips parted, the bright inner sea would ebb, and there the faces would be again, more intense than ever. With a shudder of shame I'd hide my face on her shoulder and in the warm darkness there, while a frill of her prissy collar gently scratched my nose, I felt united with Hitler and all the villains, traitors, madmen, and failures who had managed to keep, up to the moment of capture or death, a woman with them. This had puzzled me. In high school females were proud and remote; in the newspapers they were fantastic monsters of submission. And now Molly administered reassurance to me with small motions and bodily adjustments that had about them a strange flavor of the practical.

Our parents met us at the station. I was startled at how tired my mother looked. There were deep blue dents on either side of her nose, and her hair seemed somehow dissociated from her head, as if it were a ragged, half-gray wig she had put on carelessly. She was a heavy woman and her weight, which she usually carried upright, like a kind of wealth, had slumped away from her ownership and seemed, in the sullen light of the railway platform, to weigh on the world. I asked, "How's Grandpa?" He had taken to bed several months before with pains in his chest.

"He still sings," she said rather sharply. For entertainment in his increasing blindness my grandfather had long ago begun to sing, and his shapely old voice would pour forth hymns, forgotten comic ballads, and camp-meeting songs at any hour. His memory seemed to improve the longer he lived.

My mother's irritability was more manifest in the private cavity of the car; her heavy silence oppressed me. "You look so tired, Mother," I said, trying to take the offensive.

"That's nothing to how you look," she answered. "What happened up there? You stoop like an old married man."

"Nothing happened," I lied. My cheeks were parched, as if her high steady anger had the power of giving sunburn.

"I remember that Bingaman girl's mother when we first moved to town. She was the smuggest little snip south of the pike. They're real old Olinger stock, you know. They have no use for hillbillies."

My father tried to change the subject. "Well, you won one debate, Allen, and that's more than I would have done. I don't see how you do it."

"Why, he gets it from you, Victor. I've never won a debate with you."

"He gets it from Pop Baer. If that man had gone into politics, Lillian, all the misery of his life would have been avoided."

"Dad was never a debater. He was a bully. Don't go with little women, Allen. It puts you too close to the ground."

"I'm not *going* with *any*body, Mother. Really, you're so fanciful."

"Why, when she stepped off the train from the way her chins bounced I thought she had eaten a canary. And then making my poor son, all skin and bones, carry her bag. When she walked by me I honestly was afraid she'd spit in my eye."

"I had to carry somebody's bag. I'm sure she doesn't know who you are." Though it was true I had talked a good deal about my family the night before.

My mother turned away from me. "You see, Victor—he defends her. When I was his age that girl's mother gave me a cut I'm still bleeding from, and my own son attacks me on behalf of her fat little daughter. I wonder if her mother put her up to catching him."

"Molly's a nice girl," my father interceded. "She never gave me any trouble in class like some of those smug bastards." But he was curiously listless, for so Christian a man, in pronouncing this endorsement.

I discovered that nobody wanted me to go with Molly Bingaman. My friends—for on the strength of being funny I did have some friends, classmates whose love affairs went on over my head but whom I could accompany, as clown, on communal outings—never talked with me about Molly, and when I brought her to their parties gave the impression of ignoring her, so that I stopped taking her. Teachers at school would smile an odd tight smile when they saw me leaning by her locker or hanging around in the stairways. The eleventh-grade English instructor—one of my "boosters" on the faculty, a man who was always trying to "challenge" me, to "exploit" my "potential"—took me aside and told me how stupid she was. She just couldn't grasp the logical principals of syntax. He confided her parsing mistakes to me as if they betrayed—as indeed in a way they did—an obtuseness her social manner cleverly concealed. Even the Fabers, an ultra-Republican couple who ran a luncheonette near the high school, showed malicious delight whenever Molly and I broke up, and persistently treated my attachment as being a witty piece of play, like my pretense with Mr. Faber of being a Communist. The entire town seemed ensnarled in my mother's myth, that escape was my proper fate. It was as if I were a sport that the ghostly elders of Olinger had segregated from the rest of the livestock and agreed to donate in time to the air; this fitted with the ambiguous sensation I had always had in the town, of being simultaneously flattered and rejected.

Molly's parents disapproved because in their eyes my family was virtually white trash. It was so persistently hammered into me that I was too good for Molly that I scarcely considered the proposition that, by another scale, she was too good for me. Further, Molly herself shielded me. Only once, exasperated by some tedious, condescending confession of mine, did she state that her mother didn't like me. "Why not?" I asked, genuinely surprised. I admired Mrs. Bingaman —she was beautifully preserved—and I always felt gay in her house, with its white woodwork and matching furniture and vases of iris posing before polished mirrors.

"Oh, I don't know. She thinks you're flippant."

"But that's not true. Nobody takes himself more seriously than I do."

While Molly protected me from the Bingaman side of the ugliness, I conveyed the Dow side more or less directly to her. It infuriated me that nobody allowed me to be proud of her. I kept, in effect, asking her, Why was she stupid in English? Why didn't she get along with my friends? Why did she look so dumpy and smug?—this last despite the fact that she often, especially in intimate moments, looked beautiful to me. I was especially angry with her because this affair had brought out an ignoble, hysterical, brutal aspect of my mother that I might never have had to see otherwise. I had hoped to keep things secret from her, but even if her intuition had not been relentless, my father, at school, knew everything. Sometimes, indeed, my mother said that she didn't care if I went with Molly; it was my father who was upset. Like a frantic dog tied by one leg, she snapped in any direction, mouthing ridiculous fancies—such as that Mrs. Bingaman had sicked Molly on me just to keep me from going to college and giving the Dows something to be proud of—that would make us both suddenly start laughing. Laughter in that house that winter had a guilty sound. My grandfather was dying, and lay upstairs singing and coughing and weeping as the mood came to him, and we were too poor to hire a nurse, and too kind and cowardly to send him to a "home." It was still his house, after all. Any noise he made seemed to slash my mother's heart, and she was unable to sleep upstairs near him, and waited the nights out on the sofa downstairs. In her desperate state she would say unforgivable things to me even while the tears streamed down her face. I've never seen so many tears as I saw that winter.

Every time I saw my mother cry, it seemed I had to make Molly cry. I developed a skill at it; it came naturally to an only child who had been surrounded all his life by adults ransacking each other for the truth. Even in the heart of intimacy, half-naked each of us, I would say something to humiliate her. We never made love in the final, coital sense. My reason was a mixture of idealism and superstition; I felt that if I took her virginity she would be mine forever. I depended overmuch on a technicality; she gave herself to me anyway, and I had her anyway, and have her still, for the longer I travel in a direction I could not have taken with her, the more clearly she seems the one person who loved me without advantage. I was a homely, comically ambitious hillbilly, and I even refused to tell her I loved her, to pronounce the word "love"—an icy piece of pedantry that shocks me now that I have almost forgotten the context of confusion in which it seemed wise.

In addition to my grandfather's illness, and my mother's grief, and my waiting to hear if I had won a scholarship to the one college that seemed good enough for me, I was burdened with managing too many petty affairs of my graduating class. I was in charge of yearbook writeups, art editor of the school paper, chairman of the Class Gift Committee, director of the Senior ..... ably, and teachers' workhorse. Frightened by my father's tales of nervous breakdowns he had seen, I kept listening for the sounds of my brain snapping, and the image of that gray, infinitely interconnected mass seemed to extend outward, to become my whole world, one dense organic dungeon, and I felt I had to get out; if I could just get out of this, into June, it would be blue sky, and I would be all right for life.

One Friday night in spring, after trying for over an hour to write thirty-five affectionate words for the yearbook about a null girl in the Secretarial Course I had never spoken a word to, I heard my grandfather begin coughing upstairs with a sound like dry membrane tearing, and I panicked. I called up the stairs, "Mother! I must go out."

"It's nine-thirty."

"I know, but I have to. I'm going insane."

Without waiting to hear her answer or to find a coat, I left the house and got our old car out of the garage. The weekend before, I had broken up with Molly again. All week I hadn't spoken to her, though I had seen her once in Faber's, with a boy in her class, averting her face while I, hanging by the side of the pinball machine, made wisecracks in her direction. I didn't dare go up to her door and knock so late at night; I just parked across the street and watched the lit windows of her house. Through their living-room window I could see one of Mrs. Bingaman's vases of hothouse iris standing on a white mantel, and my open car window admitted the spring air, which delicately smelled of wet ashes. Molly was probably out on a date with that moron in her class. But then the Bingamans' door opened, and her figure appeared in the rectangle of light. Her back was toward me,

a coat was on her arm, and ⸻ mother seemed to be screaming. Molly closed the door and ran down off the porch and
across the street and quickly got into the car, her eyes downcast in their sockets of shadow. *She came.* When I have finally
forgotten everything else, her powdery fragrance, her lucid
cool skin, the way her lower lip was like a curved pillow of
two cloths, the dusty red outer and wet pink inner, I'll still
be grieved by this about Molly, that she came to me.

After I returned her to her house—she told me not to
worry, her mother enjoyed shouting—I went to the all-night
diner just beyond the Olinger town line and ate three hamburgers, ordering them one at a time, and drank two glasses
of milk. It was close to two o'clock when I got home, but my
mother was still awake. She lay on the sofa in the dark, with
the radio sitting on the floor murmuring Dixieland piped
up from New Orleans by way of Philadelphia. Radio music
was a steady feature of her insomniac life; not only did it
help drown out the noise of her father upstairs but she
seemed to enjoy it in itself. She would resist my father's
pleas to come to bed by saying that the New Orleans pro-
gram was not over yet. The radio was an old Philco we had
always had; I had once drawn a fish on the orange disc of
its celluloid dial, which looked to my child's eyes like a
fishbowl.

Her loneliness caught at me; I went into the living room
and sat on a chair with my back to the window. For a long
time she looked at me tensely out of the darkness. "Well,"
she said at last, "how was little hotpants?" The vulgarity this
affair had brought out in her language appalled me.

"I made her cry," I told her.

"Why do you torment the girl?"

"To please you."

"It doesn't please me."

"Well, then, stop nagging me."

"I'll stop nagging you if you'll solemnly tell me you're
willing to marry her."

I said nothing to this, and after waiting she went on in
a different voice, "Isn't it funny, that you should show this
weakness?"

"Weakness is a funny way to put it when it's the only
thing that gives me strength."

"Does it really, Allen? Well. It may be. I forget, you were
born here."

Upstairs, close to our heads, my grandfather, in a voice frail but still melodious, began to sing, "There is a happy land, far, far away, where saints in glory stand, bright, bright as day." We listened; and his voice broke into coughing, a terrible rending cough growing in fury, struggling to escape, and loud with fear he called my mother's name. She didn't stir. His voice grew enormous, a bully's voice, as he repeated, "Lillian! Lillian!" and I saw my mother's shape quiver with the force coming down the stairs into her; she was like a dam; and then the power, as my grandfather fell momentarily silent, flowed toward me in the darkness, and I felt intensely angry, and hated that black mass of suffering, even while I realized, with a rapid, light calculation, that I was too weak to withstand it.

In a dry tone of certainty and dislike—how hard my heart had become.—I told her, "All right. You'll win this one, Mother; but it'll be the last one you'll win."

My pang of fright following this unprecedentedly cold insolence seemed to blot my senses; the chair ceased to be felt under me, and the walls and furniture of the room fell away—there was only the dim orange glow of the radio dial down below. In a husky voice that seemed to come across a great distance my mother said, with typical melodrama, "Goodbye, Allen."

Should Wizard Hit Mommy?

IN THE EVENINGS and for Saturday naps like today's, Jack told his daughter Jo a story out of his head. This custom, begun when she was two, was itself now nearly two years old, and his head felt empty. Each new story was a slight variation of a basic tale: a small creature, usually named Roger (Roger Fish, Roger Squirrel, Roger Chipmunk), had some problem and went with it to the wise old owl. The owl told him to go to the wizard, and the wizard performed a magic spell that solved the problem, demanding in payment a number of pennies greater than the number Roger Creature had but in the same breath directing the animal to a place where the extra pennies could be found. Then Roger was so happy he played many games with other creatures, and went home to his mother just in time to hear the train whistle that brought his daddy home from Boston. Jack described their supper, and the story was over. Working his way through this scheme was especially fatiguing on Saturday, because Jo never fell asleep in naps any more, and knowing this made the rite seem futile.

The little girl (not so little any more; the bumps her feet made under the covers were halfway down the bed, their big double bed that they let her be in for naps and when she was sick) had at last arranged herself, and from the way her fat face deep in the pillow shone in the sunlight sifting through the drawn shades, it did not seem fantastic that something magic would occur, and she would take her nap like an infant of two. Her brother, Bobby, was two, and already asleep with his bottle. Jack asked, "Who shall the story be about today?"

"Roger . . ." Jo squeezed her eyes shut and smiled to be thinking she was thinking. Her eyes opened, her mother's blue. "Skunk," she said firmly.

57

A new animal; they must talk about skunks at nursery school. Having a fresh hero momentarily stirred Jack to creative enthusiasm. "All right," he said. "Once upon a time, in the deep dark woods, there was a tiny little creature name of Roger Skunk. And he smelled very bad—"

"Yes," Jo said.

"He smelled so bad none of the other little woodland creatures would play with him." Jo looked at him solemnly; she hadn't foreseen this. "Whenever he would go out to play," Jack continued with zest, remembering certain humiliations of his own childhood, "all of the other tiny animals would cry, 'Uh-oh, here comes Roger Stinky Skunk,' and they would run away, and Roger Skunk would stand there all alone, and two little round tears would fall from his eyes." The corners of Jo's mouth drooped down and her lower lip bent forward as he traced with a forefinger along the side of her nose the course of one of Roger Skunk's tears.

"Won't he see the owl?" she asked in a high and faintly roughened voice.

Sitting on the bed beside her, Jack felt the covers tug as her legs switched tensely. He was pleased with this moment —he was telling her something true, something she must know—and had no wish to hurry on. But downstairs a chair scraped, and he realized he must get down to help Clare paint the living-room woodwork.

"Well, he walked along very sadly and came to a very big tree, and in the tiptop of the tree was an enormous wise old owl."

"Good."

" 'Mr. Owl,' Roger Skunk said, 'all the other little animals run away from me because I smell so bad.' 'So you do,' the owl said. 'Very, very bad.' 'What can I do?' Roger Skunk said, and he cried very hard."

"The wizard, the wizard," Jo shouted, and sat right up, and a Little Golden Book spilled from the bed.

"Now, Jo. Daddy's telling the story. Do you want to tell Daddy the story?"

"No. You tell me."

"Then lie down and be sleepy."

Her head relapsed onto the pillow and she said, "Out of your head."

"Well. The owl thought and thought. At last he said, 'Why don't you go see the wizard?' "

"Daddy?"

"What?"

"Are magic spells *real?*" This was a new phase, just this last month, a reality phase. When he told her spiders eat bugs, she turned to her mother and asked, "Do they *really?*" and when Clare told her God was in the sky and all around them, she turned to her father and insisted, with a sly yet eager smile, "Is He *really?*"

"They're real in stories," Jack answered curtly. She had made him miss a beat in the narrative. "The owl said, 'Go through the dark woods, under the apple trees, into the swamp, over the crick—' "

"What's a crick?"

"A little river. 'Over the crick, and there will be the wizard's house.' And that's the way Roger Skunk went, and pretty soon he came to a little white house, and he rapped on the door." Jack rapped on the window sill, and under the covers Jo's tall figure clenched in an infantile thrill. "And then a tiny little old man came out, with a long white beard and a pointed blue hat, and said, 'Eh? Whatzis? Whatcher want? You smell awful.' " The wizard's voice was one of Jack's own favorite effects; he did it by scrunching up his face and somehow whining through his eyes, which felt for the interval rheumy. He felt being an old man suited him.

" 'I know it,' Roger Skunk said, 'and all the little animals run away from me. The enormous wise owl said you could help me.'

" 'Eh? Well, maybe. Come on in. Don't git too close.' Now, inside, Jo, there were all these magic things, all jumbled together in a big dusty heap, because the wizard did not have any cleaning lady."

"Why?"

"Why? Because he was a wizard, and a very old man."

"Will he die?"

"No. Wizards don't die. Well, he rummaged around and found an old stick called a magic wand and asked Roger Skunk what he wanted to smell like. Roger thought and thought and said, 'Roses.' "

"Yes. Good," Jo said smugly.

Jack fixed her with a trancelike gaze and chanted in the wizard's elderly irritable voice:

> " 'Abracadabry, hocus-poo,
> Roger Skunk, how do you do,
> Roses, boses, pull an ear,

Roger Skunk, you never fear:
        Bingo!' "

He paused as a rapt expression widened out from his daughter's nostrils, forcing her eyebrows up and her lower lip down in a wide noiseless grin, an expression in which Jack was startled to recognize his wife feigning pleasure at cocktail parties. "And all of a sudden," he whispered, "the whole inside of the wizard's house was full of the smell of— *roses!* 'Roses!' Roger Fish cried. And the wizard said, very cranky, 'That'll be seven pennies.' "

"Daddy."

"What?"

"Roger *Skunk*. You said Roger Fish."

"Yes. Skunk."

"You said Roger *Fish*. Wasn't that silly?"

"Very silly of your stupid old daddy. Where was I? Well, you know about the pennies."

"Say it."

"O.K. Roger Skunk said, 'But all I have is four pennies,' and he began to cry." Jo made the crying face again, but this time without a trace of sincerity. This annoyed Jack. Downstairs some more furniture rumbled. Clare shouldn't move heavy things; she was six months pregnant. It would be their third.

"So the wizard said, 'Oh, very well. Go to the end of the lane and turn around three times and look down the magic well and there you will find three pennies. Hurry up.' So Roger Skunk went to the end of the lane and turned around three times and there in the magic well were *three pennies!* So he took them back to the wizard and was very happy and ran out into the woods and all the other little animals gathered around him because he smelled so good. And they played tag, baseball, football, basketball, lacrosse, hockey, soccer, and pick-up-sticks,"

"What's pick-up-sticks?"

"It's a game you play with sticks."

"Like the wizard's magic wand?"

"Kind of. And they played games and laughed all afternoon and then it began to get dark and they all ran home to their mommies."

Jo was starting to fuss with her hands and look out of the window, at the crack of day that showed under the shade. She thought the story was all over. Jack didn't like women

when they took anything for ranted; he liked them apprehensive, hanging on his words. "Now, Jo, are you listening?"

"Yes."

"Because this is very interesting. Roger Skunk's mommy
said. 'What's that awful smell?' "

"Wha-at?"

"And Roger Skunk said, 'It's me, Mommy. I smell like
roses.' And she said, 'Who made you smell like that?' And
he said, 'The wizard,' and she said, 'Well, of all the nerve.
You come with me and we're going right back to that very
awful wizard.' "

Jo sat up, her hands dabbling in the air with genuine
fright. "But Daddy, then he said about the other little aminals
run *away!*" Her hands skittered off, into the underbrush.

"All right. He said, 'But Mommy, all the other little animals run away,' and she said, 'I don't care. You smelled the
way a little skunk should have and I'm going to take you
right back to that wizard,' and she took an umbrella and
went back with Roger Skunk and hit that wizard right over
the head."

"No," Jo said, and put her hand out to touch his lips, yet
even in her agitation did not quite dare to stop the source
of truth. Inspiration came to her. "Then the wizard hit *her*
on the head and did not change that little skunk back."

"No," he said. "The wizard said 'O.K.' and Roger Skunk
did not smell of roses any more. He smelled very bad again."

"But the other little amum—*oh!*—amum—"

"Joanne. It's Daddy's story. Shall Daddy not tell you any
more stories?" Her broad face looked at him through sifted
light, astounded. "This is what happened, then. Roger Skunk
and his mommy went home and they heard *Woo-oo, woooo-oo*
and it was the choo-choo train bringing Daddy Skunk home
from Boston. And they had lima beans, pork chops, celery,
liver, mashed potatoes, and Pie-Oh-My for dessert. And when
Roger Skunk was in bed Mommy Skunk came up and hugged
him and said he smelled like her little baby skunk again
and she loved him very much. And that's the end of the
story."

"But Daddy."

"What?"

"Then did the other little ani-mals run away?"

"No, because eventually they got used to the way he was
and did not mind it at all."

"What's evenshiladee?"

"In a little while."

"That was a stupid mommy."

"It was *not*," he said with rare emphasis, and believed, from her expression, that she realized he was defending his own mother to her, or something as odd. "Now I want you to put your big heavy head in the pillow and have a good long nap." He adjusted the shade so not even a crack of day showed, and tiptoed to the door, in the pretense that she was already asleep. But when he turned, she was crouching on top of the covers and staring at him. "Hey. Get under the covers and fall faaast asleep. Bobby's asleep."

She stood up and bounced gingerly on the springs. "Daddy."

"What?"

"Tomorrow, I want you to tell me the story that that wizard took that magic wand and hit that mommy"—her plump arms chopped fiercely—"right over the head."

"No. That's not the story. The point is that the little skunk loved his mommy more than he loved aaalll the other animals and she knew what was right."

"No. Tomorrow you say he hit that mommy. Do it." She kicked her legs up and sat down on the bed with a great heave and complaint of springs, as she had done hundreds of times before, except that this time she did not laugh. "Say it, Daddy."

"Well, we'll see. Now at least have a rest. Stay on the bed. You're a good girl."

He closed the door and went downstairs. Clare had spread the newspapers and opened the paint can and, wearing an old shirt of his on top of her maternity smock, was stroking the chair rail with a dipped brush. Above him footsteps vibrated and he called, "*Joanne.* Shall I come up there and spank you?" The footsteps hesitated.

"That was a long story," Clare said.

"The poor kid," he answered, and with utter weariness watched his wife labor. The woodwork, a cage of moldings and rails and baseboards all around them, was half old tan and half new ivory and he felt caught in an ugly middle position, and though he as well felt his wife's presence in the cage with him, he did not want to speak with her, work with her, touch her, anything.

A Sense of Shelter

SNOW fell against the high school all day, wet big-flaked snow that did not accumulate well. Sharpening two pencils, William looked down on a parking lot that was a blackboard in reverse, car tires had cut smooth arcs of black into the white, and wherever a school bus had backed around, it had left an autocratic signature of two *V*'s. The snow, though at moments it whirled opaquely, could not quite bleach these scars away. The temperature must be exactly 32°. The window was open a crack, and a canted pane of glass lifted outdoor air into his face, coating the cedarwood scent of pencil shavings with the transparent odor of the wet window sill. With each revolution of the handle his knuckles came within a fraction of an inch of the tilted glass, and the faint chill this proximity breathed on them sharpened his already acute sense of shelter.

The sky behind the shreds of snow was stone-colored. The murk inside the high classroom gave the air a solidity that limited the overhead radiance to its own vessels; six globes of dull incandescence floated on the top of a thin sea. The feeling the gloom gave him was not gloomy but joyous: he felt they were all sealed in, safe; the colors of cloth were dyed deeper, the sound of whispers was made more distinct, the smells of tablet paper and wet shoes and varnish and face powder pierced him with a vivid sense of possession. These were his classmates sealed in, his, the stupid as well as the clever, the plain as well as the lovely, his enemies as well as his friends, his. He felt like a king and seemed to move to his seat between the bowed heads of subjects that loved him less than he loved them. His seat was sanctioned by tradition; for twelve years he had sat at the rear of classrooms, William Young, flanked by Marsha Wyckoff and Andy Zimmerman. Once there had been two Zimmermans, but one went to work in his father's greenhouse, and in some classes—Latin and Trig—there were none, and William sat at the edge of the class as if on the lip of a cliff, and Marsha Wyck-off became Marvin Wolf or Sandra Wade, but it was always the same desk, whose surface altered from hour to hour but from whose blue-stained ink-hole his mind could extract, like a chain of magicians' handkerchiefs, a continuity of years. As a senior he was a kind of king, and as a teacher's pet another kind, a puppet king, who gathered in appointive posts and even, when the moron vote split between two football heroes, some elective ones. He was not popular, he had never had a girl, his intense friends of childhood had drifted off into teams and gangs, and in large groups—when the whole school, for instance, went in the fall to the beautiful, dung-and-cotton-candy-smelling county fair—he was always an odd man, without a seat on the bus home. But exclusion is itself a form of inclusion. He even had a nickname: Mip, because he stuttered. Taunts no longer much frightened him; he had come late into his physical inheritance, but this summer it had arrived, and he at last stood equal with his enormous, boisterous parents, and had to unbutton his shirt cuffs to get his wrists through them, and discovered he could pick up a basketball with one hand. So, his long legs blocking two aisles, he felt regal even in size and, almost trembling with happiness under the high globes of light beyond whose lunar glow invisible snowflakes were drowning on the gravel roof of his castle, believed that the long delay of unpopularity had been merely a consolidation, that he was at last strong enough to make his move. Today he would tell Mary Landis he loved her.

He had loved her ever since, a fat-faced tomboy with freckles and green eyes, she deftly stole his rubber-lined schoolbag on the walk back from second grade along Jewett Street and outran him—simply had better legs. The superior speed a boy was supposed to have failed to come; his kidneys burned with panic. In front of the grocery store next to her home she stopped and turned. She was willing to have him catch up. This humiliation on top of the rest was too much to bear. Tears broke in his throat; he spun around and ran home and threw himself on the floor of the front parlor, where his grandfather, feet twiddling, perused the newspaper and soliloquized all morning. In time the letter slot rustled, and the doorbell rang, and Mary gave his mother the schoolbag and the two of them politely exchanged whispers. Their voices had been to him, lying there on the carpet with his head wrapped in his arms, indistinguishable. Mother had always liked Mary. From when she had been a tiny girl dancing along the hedge on the end of an older sister's arm, Mother had liked her. Out of all the children that flocked, similar as pigeons, through the neighborhood, Mother's heart had reached out with claws and fastened on Mary. He never took the schoolbag to school again, had refused to touch it. He supposed it was still in the attic, still faintly smelling of sweet pink rubber.

Fixed high on the plaster like a wren clinging to a barn wall, the buzzer sounded the two-minute signal. In the middle of the classroom Mary Landis stood up, a Monitor badge pinned to her belly. Her broad red belt was buckled with a brass bow and arrow. She wore a lavender sweater with the sleeves pushed up to expose her forearms, a delicately cheap effect. Wild stories were told about her; perhaps it was merely his knowledge of these that put the hardness in her face. Her eyes seemed braced for squinting and their green was frosted. Her freckles had faded. William thought she laughed less this year; now that she was in the Secretarial Course and he in the College Preparatory, he saw her in only one class a day, this one, English. She stood a second, eclipsed at the thighs by Jack Stephens' zebra-striped shoulders, and looked back at the class with a stiff worn glance, as if she had seen the same faces too many times before. Her habit of perfect posture emphasized the angularity she had grown into. There was a nervous edge, a boxiness in her bones, that must have been waiting all along under the childish fat. Her eye sockets were deeply indented and her chin had a prim square set that seemed in the murky air tremulous and defiant. Her skirt was cut square and straight. Below the waist she was lean; the legs that had outrun him were still athletic; she starred at hockey and cheerleading. Above, she was abundant: so stacked her spine curved backwards to keep her body balanced. She turned and in switching up the aisle encountered a boy's leg thrown into her path. She coolly looked down until it withdrew. She was used to such attentions. Her pronged chest poised, Mary proceeded out the door, and someone she saw in the hall made her smile, a wide smile full of warmth and short white teeth, and love scooped at William's heart. He would tell her.

In another minute, the second bell rasped. Shuffling through the perfumed crowds to his next class, he crooned to himself

in the slow, over-enunciated manner of the Negro vocalist
who had brought the song back this year:

> "Lah-vender blue, dilly dilly,
> Lavendih gree-heen;
> *Eef* I were king, dilly dilly,
> You would: be queen."

The song gave him an exultant sliding sensation that inter-
twined with the pleasures of his day. He knew all the answers,
he had done all the work, the teachers called upon him only
to rebuke the ignorance of the others. In Trig and Soc Sci both
it was this way. In gym, the fourth hour of the morning, he,
who was always picked near the last, startled his side by
excelling at volleyball, leaping like a madman, shouting like
a bully. The bàll felt light as a feather against his big bones.
His hair in wet quills from the shower, he walked in the icy
air to Luke's Luncheonette, where he ate three hamburgers in
a booth with three juniors. There was Barry Kruppman, a tall,
thyroid-eyed boy who came on the school bus from the country town of Bowsville and who was an amateur hypnotist; he
told the tale of a Portland, Oregon, businessman who under
hypnosis had been taken back through sixteen reincarnations
to the condition of an Egyptian concubine in the household
of a hign priest of Isis. There was his friend Lionel Griffin,
a pudgy simp whose blond hair puffed out above his ears in
two slick waxed wings. He was rumored to be a fairy, and in
fact did seem most excited by the transvestite aspect of the
soul's transmigration. And there was Lionel's girl Virginia, a
drab little mystery who chain-smoked Herbert Tareytons and
never said anything. She had sallow skin and smudged eyes
and Lionel kept jabbing her and shrieking, making William
wince. He would rather have sat with members of his own
class, who filled the other booths, but he would have had to
force himself on them. These juniors admired him and welcomed his company. He asked, "Wuh-well, was he ever a
c-c-c-cockroach, like Archy?"

Kruppman's face grew intense; his furry lids dropped
down over the bulge of his eyes, and when they drew back,
his pupils were as small and hard as BBs. "That's the really
interesting thing. There was this gap, see, between his being
a knight under Charlemagne and then a sailor on a ship putting out from Macedonia—that's where Yugoslavia is now—
in the time of Nero; there was this gap, when the only thing

the guy would do was walk around the office snarling and growling, see, like this." Kruppman worked his blotched ferret face up into a snarl and Griffin shrieked. "He tried to bite one of the assistants and they think that for six hundred years" —the uncanny, unhealthy seriousness of his whisper hushed Griffin momentarily—"for six hundred years he just was a series of wolves. Probably in the German forests. You see, when he was in Macedonia"—his whisper barely audible—"he murdered a woman."

Griffin squealed in ecstasy and cried, "Oh, Kruppman! Kruppman, how you do go on!" and jabbed Virginia in the arm so hard a Herbert Tareyton jumped from her hand and bobbled across the Formica table. William gazed over their heads in pain.

The crowds at the soda counter had thinned so that when the door to the outside opened he saw Mary come in and hesitate there for a second where the smoke inside and the snow outside swirled together. The mixture made a kind of— Kruppman's ridiculous story had put the phrase in his head —wolf-weather, and she was just a gray shadow caught in it alone. She bought a pack of cigarettes from Luke and went out again, a kerchief around her head, the pneumatic thing above the door hissing behind her. For a long time, always in fact, she had been at the center of whatever gang was the one: in the second grade the one that walked home up Jewett Street together, and in the sixth grade the one that went bicycling as far away as the quarry and the Rentschler estate and played touch football Saturday afternoons, and in the ninth grade the one that went roller-skating at Candlebridge Park with the tenth-grade boys, and in the eleventh grade the one that held parties lasting past midnight and that on Sundays drove in caravans as far as Philadelphia and back. And all the while there had been a succession of boy friends, first Jack Stephens and Fritz March in their class and then boys a grade ahead and then Barrel Lord, who was a senior when they were sophomores and whose name was in the newspapers all football season, and then this last summer someone out of the school altogether, a man she met while working as a waitress in the city of Alton. So this year her weekends were taken up, and the party gang carried on as if she had never existed, and nobody saw her much except in school and when she stopped by in Luke's to buy a pack of cigarettes. Her silhouette against the big window had looked wan, her head hooded, her face nibbled by light, her fingers fiddling

on the veined counter with her coins. He yearned to reach
out, to comfort her, but he was wedged deep in the shrill
booths, between the jingling guts of the pinball machine and
the hillbilly joy of the jukebox. The impulse left him with a
disagreeable feeling. He had loved her too long to want to
pity her; it endangered the investment of worship on which
he had not yet realized any return.

The two hours of the school afternoon held Latin and a
study hall. In study hall, while the five people at the table
with him played tic-tac-toe and sucked cough drops and
yawned, he did all his homework for the next day. He prepared thirty lines of Vergil, Aeneas in the Underworld. The
study hall was a huge low room in the basement of the building; its coziness crept into Tartarus. On the other side of the
fudge-colored wall the circular saw in the woodworking shop
whined and gasped and then whined again; it bit off pieces of
wood with a rising, somehow terrorized inflection—*bzzzzzup!*
He solved ten problems in trigonometry. His mind cut neatly
through their knots and separated them, neat stiff squares of
answer, one by one from the long but finite plank of problems that connected Plane Geometry with Solid. Lastly, as the
snow on a ragged slant drifted down into the cement pits
outside the steel-mullioned windows, he read a short story
by Edgar Allan Poe. He closed the book softly on the pleasing
sonority of its final note of horror, gazed at the red, wet,
menthol-scented inner membrane of Judy Whipple's yawn,
rimmed with flaking pink lipstick, and yielded his conscience
to the snug sense of his work done, of the snow falling, of
the warm minutes that walked through their shelter so slowly.
The perforated acoustic tiling above his head seemed the
lining of a long tube that would go all the way: high school
merging into college, college into graduate school, graduate
school into teaching at a college—section man, assistant,
associate, *full* professor, possessor of a dozen languages and a
thousand books, a man brilliant in his forties, wise in his fifties,
renowned in his sixties, revered in his seventies, and then
retired, sitting in the study lined with acoustical books until
the time came for the last transition from silence to silence,
and he would die, like Tennyson, with a copy of *Cymbeline*
beside him on the moon-drenched bed.

After school he had to go to Room 101 and cut a sports
cartoon into a stencil for the school paper. He liked the
building best when it was nearly empty, when the casual residents—the rural commuters, the do-nothings, the trash—had

cleared out. Then the janitors went down the halls sowing seeds of red wax and making an immaculate harvest with broad brooms, gathering all the fluff and hairpins and wrappers and powder that the animals had dropped that day. The basketball team thumped in the hollow gymnasium; the cheerleaders rehearsed behind drawn curtains on the stage. In Room 101 two empty-headed typists with stripes bleached into their hair banged away between giggles and mistakes. At her desk Mrs. Gregory, the faculty sponsor, wearily passed her pencil through misspelled news copy on tablet paper. William took the shadow box from the top of the filing cabinet and the styluses and little square plastic shading screens from their drawer and the stencil from the closet where the typed stencils hung, like fragile scarves, on hooks. B-BALLERS BOW, 57-42, was the headline. He drew a tall b-baller bowing to a stumpy pagan idol, labelled "W" for victorious Weiserton High, and traced it in the soft blue wax with the fine loop stylus. His careful breath grazed his knuckles. His eyebrows frowned while his heart bobbed happily on the giddy prattle of the typists. The shadow box was simply a black frame holding a pane of glass and lifted at one end by two legs so the light bulb, fitted in a tin tray, could slide under; it was like a primitive lean-to sheltering a fire. As he worked, his eyes smarting, he mixed himself up with the light bulb, felt himself burning under a slanting roof upon which a huge hand scratched. The glass grew hot; the danger in the job was pulling the softened wax with your damp hand, distorting or tearing the typed letters. Sometimes the center of an *o* stuck to your skin like a bit of blue confetti. But he was expert and cautious. He returned the things to their places feeling airily tall, heightened by Mrs. Gregory's appreciation, which she expressed by keeping her back turned, in effect stating that other staff members were undependable but William did not need to be watched.

In the hall outside Room 101 only the shouts of a basketball scrimmage reverberated; the chant of the cheerleaders had been silenced. Though he had done everything, he felt reluctant to leave. Neither of his parents—both worked—would be home yet, and this building was as much his home. He knew all its nooks. On the second floor of the annex, beyond the art room, there was a strange, narrow boys' lavatory that no one ever seemed to use. It was here one time that Barry Kruppman tried to hypnotize him and cure his stuttering. Kruppman's voice purred and his irises turned tiny in the bulging whites and for a moment William felt himself lean backward involuntarily, but he was distracted by the bits of bloodshot pink in the corners of these portentous eyes; the folly of giving up his will to an intellectual inferior occurred to him; he refused to let go and go under, and perhaps therefore his stuttering had continued.

The frosted window at the end of the long room cast a watery light on the green floor and made the porcelain urinals shine like slices of moon. The semi-opacity of this window gave the room's air of secrecy great density. William washed his hands with exaggerated care, enjoying the lavish amount of powdered soap provided for him in this castle. He studied his face in the mirror, making infinitesimal adjustments to attain the absolutely most flattering angle, and then put his hands below his throat to get their strong, long-fingered beauty into the picture. As he walked toward the door he sang, closing his eyes and gasping as if he were a real Negro whose entire career depended upon this recording:

> "Who—told me so, dilly dilly,
> Who told me soho?
> *Aii* told myself, dilly dilly,
> I told: me so."

When he emerged into the hall it was not empty: one girl walked down its varnished perspective toward him, Mary Landis, a scarf on her head and books in her arms. Her locker was up here, on the second floor of the annex. His own was in the annex basement. A tickling sensation that existed neither in the medium of sound nor of light crowded against his throat. She flipped the scarf back from her hair and in a conversational voice that carried well down the clean planes of the hall said, "Hi, Billy." The name came from way back, when they were both children, and made him feel small but brave.

"Hi. How are you?"

"Fine." Her smile broadened out from the *F* of this word.

What was so funny? Was she really, as it seemed, pleased to see him? "Du-did you just get through cheer-cheer-cheer-leading?"

"Yes. Thank God. *Oh* she's so awful. She makes us do the same stupid locomotives for every cheer; I told her, no wonder nobody cheers any more."

"This is M-M-Miss Potter?" He blushed, feeling that he

made an ugly face in getting past the *M*. When he got caught in the middle of a sentence the constriction was somehow worse. He admired the way words poured up her throat, distinct and petulant.

"Yes, Potbottom Potter," she said, "she's just aching for a man and takes it out on us. I wish she would get one. Honestly, Billy, I have half a mind to quit. I'll be so glad when June comes, I'll never set foot in this idiotic building again."

Her lips, pale with the lipstick worn off, crinkled bitterly. Her face, foreshortened from the height of his eyes, looked cross as a cat's. It a little shocked him that poor Miss Potter and this kind, warm school stirred her to what he had to take as actual anger; this grittiness in her was the first abrasive texture he had struck today. Couldn't she see around teachers, into their fatigue, their poverty, their fear? It had been so long since he had spoken to her, he wasn't sure how coarse she had become. "Don't quit," he brought out of his mouth at last. "It'd be n-n-n-nuh—it'd be nothing without you."

He pushed open the door at the end of the hall for her and as she passed under his arm she looked up and said, "Why, aren't you sweet?"

The stairwell, all asphalt and iron, smelled of galoshes. It felt more secret than the hall, more specially theirs; there was something magical in its shifting multiplicity of planes as they descended that lifted the spell on his tongue, so that words came as quickly as his feet pattered on the steps.

"No I mean it," he said, "you're really a beautiful cheerleader. But then you're beautiful period."

"I've skinny legs."

"Who told you that?"

"Somebody."

"Well *he* wasn't very sweet."

"No."

"Why do you hate this poor old school?"

"Now Billy. You know you don't care about this junky place any more than I do."

"I love it. It breaks my heart to hear you say you want to get out, because then I'll never see you again."

"You don't care, do you?"

"Why sure I care; you *know*"—their feet stopped; they had reached bottom, the first-floor landing, two brass-barred doors and a grimy radiator—"I've always li-loved you."

"You don't mean that."

"I do too. It's ridiculous but there it is. I wanted to tell you today and now I have."

He expected her to laugh and go out the door, but instead she showed an unforseeable willingness to discuss this awkward matter. He should have realized before this that women enjoy being talked to. "It's a very silly thing to say," she asserted tentatively.

"I don't see why," he said, fairly bold now that he couldn't seem more ridiculous, and yet picking his words with a certain strategic care. "It's not *that* silly to love somebody, I mean what the hell. Probably what's silly is not to do anything about it for umpteen years but then I never had an opportunity, I thought."

He set his books down on the radiator and she set hers down beside his. "What kind of opportunity were you waiting for?"

"Well, see, that's it; I didn't know." He wished, in a way, she would go out the door. But she had propped herself against the wall and plainly awaited more talking. "Yuh-you were such a queen and I was such a nothing and I just didn't really want to presume." It wasn't very interesting; it puzzled him that she seemed to be interested. Her face had grown quite stern, the mouth very small and thoughtful, and he made a gesture with his hands intended to release her from the bother of thinking about it; after all, it was just a disposition of his heart, nothing permanent or expensive; perhaps it was just his mother's idea anyway. Half in impatience to close the account, he asked, "Will you marry me?"

"You don't want to marry me," she said. "You're going to go on and be a great man."

He blushed in pleasure; is this how she saw him, is this how they all saw him; as worthless now, but in time a great man? Had his hopes always been on view? He dissembled, saying, "No I'm not. But anyway, you're great now. You're so pretty, Mary."

"Oh, Billy," she said, "if you were me for just one day you'd hate it."

She said this rather blankly, watching his eyes; he wished her voice had shown more misery. In his world of closed surfaces a panel, carelessly pushed, had opened, and he hung in this openness paralyzed, unable to think what to say. Nothing he could think of quite fit the abruptly immense context. The radiator cleared its throat; its heat made, in the intimate volume just this side of the doors on whose windows the snow beat limply, a provocative snugness; he supposed he should try, and stepped forward, his hands lifting toward her shoulders. Mary sidestepped between him and the radiator and put the scarf back on. She lifted the cloth like a broad plaid halo above her head and then wrapped it around her chin and knotted it so she looked, in her red galoshes and bulky coat, like a peasant woman in a movie of Europe. With her thick hair swathed, her face seemed pale and chunky, and when she recradled the books in her arms her back bent humbly under the point of the kerchief. "It's too hot in here," she said. "I've got to wait for somebody." The disconnectedness of the two statements seemed natural in the fragmented atmosphere his stops and starts had produced. She bucked the brass bar with her shoulder and the door slammed open; he followed her into the weather.

"For the person who thinks your legs are too skinny?"

"Uh-huh." As she looked up at him a snowflake caught on the lashes of one eye. She jerkily rubbed that cheek on the shoulder of her coat and stamped a foot, splashing slush. Cold water gathered on the back of his thin shirt. He put his hands in his pockets and pressed his arms against his sides to keep from shivering.

"Thuh-then you wo-won't marry me?" His wise instinct told him the only way back was by going forward, through absurdity.

"We don't know each other," she said.

"My God," he said. "Why not? I've known you since I was two."

"What do you know about me?"

This awful seriousness of hers; he must dissolve it. "That you're not a virgin." But instead of making her laugh this made her face go dead and turned it away. Like beginning to kiss her, it was a mistake; in part, he felt grateful for his mistakes. They were like loyal friends who are nevertheless embarrassing. "What do you know about *me?*" he asked, setting himself up for a finishing insult but dreading it. He hated the stiff feel of his smile between his cheeks; glimpsed, as if the snow were a mirror, how hateful he looked.

"That you're basically very nice."

Her returning good for evil blinded him to his physical discomfort, set him burning with regret. "Listen," he said, "I did love you. Let's at least get that straight."

"You never loved anybody," she said. "You don't know what it is."

"O.K." he said. "Pardon me."

"You're excused."

"You better wait in the school," he told her. "He's-eez-eez going to be a long time."

She didn't answer and walked a little distance, toeing out in the childish Dutch way common to the women in this county, along the slack cable that divided the parking lot from the softball field. One bicycle, rusted as if it had been there for years, leaned in the rack, its fenders supporting airy crescents of white.

The warmth inside the door felt heavy. William picked up his books and ran his pencil along the black ribs of the radiator before going down the stairs to his locker in the annex basement. The shadows were thick at the foot of the steps; suddenly it felt late, he must hurry and get home. He was seized by the irrational fear that they were going to lock him in. The cloistered odors of paper, sweat, and, from the woodshop at the far end of the basement hall, sawdust no longer flattered him. The tall green double lockers appeared to study him critically through the three air slits near their tops. When he opened his locker, and put his books on his shelf, below Marvin Wolf's, and removed his coat from his hook, his self seemed to crawl into the long dark space thus made vacant, the humiliated ugly, educable self. In answer to a flick of his great hand the steel door weightlessly floated shut and through the length of his body he felt so clean and free he smiled. Between now and the happy future predicted for him he had nothing, almost literally nothing, to do.

Dear Alexandros

TRANSLATION *of a letter written by Alexandros Koundouriotis, Needy Child No. 26,511 in the records of Hope, Incorporated, an international charity with headquarters in New York.*

July, 1959

Dear Mr. and Mrs. Bentley:

Dear American Parents, first of all I want to inquire about your good health, and then, if you ask me, tell you that I am keeping well, for which I thank God, and hope that it is the same with you. May God keep you always well, and grant you every happiness and joy. With great eagerness I was looking forward again this month to receiving a letter from you, but unfortunately I have again not received one. So I am worried about you, for I am longing to hear about you, dear American Parents. You show such a great interest in me, and every month I receive your help. Over here it is very hot at this time of the year, for we are in the heart of the summer. The work out in the fields is very tiring, as I hear the older people saying. As for me, when I have no work at home I go down to the sea for a swim, and enjoy the sea with my friends. For at this time of the year the sea is lovely. So much for my news. Vacations continue, until it is time for the schools to reopen, when with new strength and joy we shall begin our lessons again. Today that I am writing to you I received again the $8.00 that you sent me, for the month of July, and I thank you very much. With this money I shall buy whatever I need, and we shall also buy some flour for our bread. In closing, I send you greetings from my granny and my sister, and hope that my letter finds you in good health and joy. I shall be looking forward to receiving a letter from you, to hear about you and how you are spending your summer. I greet you with much affection.

Your son,
Alexandros

Reply from Kenneth Bentley, American Parent No. 10,638.

September 25

Dear Alexandros:

We are all sorry that you should worry about us because you have not received a letter from us. I fear we are not as regular in writing as you are, but the pretentiously named organization which delivers our letters seems to be very slow, they take about three months as far as I can tell. Perhaps they send them by way of China.

You describe the Greek summer very beautifully. It is autumn now in New York City. The sad little trees along the somewhat sad little street where I live now are turning yellow, the ones that are not already dead. The pretty girls that walk along the main streets are putting on hats again. In New York the main streets run north and south so that there is usually a sunny side and a shady side and now people cross the street to be on the sunny side because the sun is no longer too warm. The sky is very blue and some evenings, after I eat in a luncheonette or restaurant, I walk a few blocks over to the East River to watch the boats and look at Brooklyn, which is another section of this immense city.

Mrs. Bentley and I no longer live together. I had not intended to tell you this but now the sentence is typed and I see no harm in it. Perhaps already you were wondering why I am writing from New York City instead of from Greenwich. Mrs. Bentley and little Amanda and Richard all still live in our nice home in Greenwich and the last time I saw them looked very well. Amanda now is starting kindergarten and was very excited and will never wear dungarees or overalls any more but insists on wearing dresses because that is what makes little girls look nice, she thinks. This makes her mother rather angry, especially on Saturdays and Sundays when Amanda plays mostly in the dirt with the neighbor children. Richard walks very well now and does not like his sister teasing him. As who does? I go to see them once a week and pick up my mail and your last letter was one of the letters I picked up and was delighted to read. Mrs. Bentley asked me to answer it, which I was delighted to do, because she had written you the last time. In fact I do not think she did, but writing letters was one thing she was not good at, although it was her idea for us to subscribe to Hope, Incorporated, and I know she loves you very much, and was especially happy to learn that you plan to begin school with "new strength and joy."

There has been much excitement in the United States over the visit of the head of Soviet Russia, Mr. Khrushchev. He is a very talkative and self-confident man and in meeting some of our own talkative and self-confident politicians there has been some friction, much of it right on television where everybody could see. My main worry was that he would be shot but I don't think he will be shot any more. His being in the country has been a funny feeling, as if you have swallowed a penny, but the American people are so anxious for peace that they will put up with small discomforts if there is any chance it will do any good. The United States, as perhaps you will learn in school, was for many years an isolated country and there still is a perhaps childish wish that other nations, even though we are a great power, just let us alone, and then the sun will shine.

That was not a very good paragraph and perhaps the man or woman who kindly translates these letters for us will kindly omit it. I have a cold in my chest that mixes with a great deal of cigarette smoke and makes me very confused, especially after I have been sitting still for a while.

I am troubled because I imagine I hear you asking, "Then were Mr. and Mrs. Bentley, who sent me such happy letters from America, and photographs of their children, and a sweater and a jackknife at Christmas, telling lies? Why do they not live together any more?" I do not wish you to worry. Perhaps in your own village you have husbands and wives who quarrel. Perhaps they quarrel but continue to live together but in America where we have so much plumbing and fast automobiles and rapid highways we have forgotten how to live with inconveniences, although I admit that my present mode of life is something of an inconvenience to me. Or perhaps in your schooling, if you keep at it, and I hope you will, the priests or nuns will have you read the very great Greek poem the *Iliad,* in which the poet Homer tells of Helen who left her husband to live with Paris among the Trojans. It is something like that with the Bentleys, except that I, a man, have gone to live among the Trojans, leaving my wife at home. I do not know if the *Iliad* is a part of your schooling, and would be curious to know. Your nation should be very proud of producing masterpieces which the whole world can enjoy. In the United States the great writers produce works which people do not enjoy, because they are so depressing to read.

But we were not telling lies, Mrs. Bentley and Amanda and Richard and I were very happy and to a degree are yet. Please continue to send us your wonderful letters, they will go to Greenwich, and we will all enjoy them. We will continue to send you the money for which you say you are grateful, though the money we give you this way is not a fourth of the money we used to spend for alcoholic drinks. Not that Mrs. Bentley and I drank all these alcoholic drinks. We had many friends who helped us, most of them very tedious people, although perhaps you would like them more than I do. Certainly they would like you more than they liked me.

I am so happy that you live near the sea where you can swim and relax from the tiring work of the fields. I was born far inland in America, a thousand miles from any ocean, and did not come to love the sea until I was grown up and married. So in that sense you are luckier than I. Certainly to be near the sea is a great blessing, and I remember often thinking how nice it was that my own children should know what it was to run on the sand of the pretty though not large beach at Greenwich, and to have that great calm horizon over their shoulders.

Now I must end, for I have agreed to take a young woman out to dinner, a young woman who, you will be interested to hear, is herself Greek in origin, though born in America, and who has much of the beauty of your race. But I have already cruelly burdened our translator. My best wishes to your granny, who has taken such good care of you since your mother died, and to your sister, whose welfare and good health is such a large concern in your heart.

Sincerely,
Kenneth Bentley

P.S.: In looking back at the beginning of my letter I see with regret that I have been unkind to the excellent organization which has made possible our friendship with you, which has produced your fine letters, which we are always happy to receive and which we read and reread. If we have not written as often as we should have it is our fault and we ask you to forgive us.

Wife-wooing

OH MY LOVE. Yes. Here we sit, on warm broad floorboards, before a fire, the children between us, in a crescent, eating. The girl and I share one half-pint of French fried potatoes; you and the boy share another; and in the center, sharing nothing, making simple reflections within himself like a jewel, the baby, mounted in an Easybaby, sucks at his bottle with frowning mastery, his selfish, contemplative eyes stealing glitter from the center of the flames. And you. You. You allow your skirt, the same black skirt in which this morning you with woman's soft bravery mounted a bicycle and sallied forth to play hymns in difficult keys on the Sunday school's old piano—you allow this black skirt to slide off your raised knees down your thighs, slide *up* your thighs in your body's absolute geography, so the parallel whiteness of their undersides is exposed to the fire's warmth and to my sight. Oh. There is a line of Joyce. I try to recover it from the legendary, imperfectly explored grottoes of *Ulysses:* a garter snapped, to please Blazes Boylan, in a deep Dublin den. What? Smackwarm. That was the crucial word. Smacked smackwarm on her smackable warm woman's thigh. Something like that. A splendid man, to feel that. Smackwarm woman's. Splendid also to feel the curious and potent, inexplicable and irrefutably magical life language leads within itself. What soul took thought and knew that adding "wo" to man would make a woman? The difference exactly. The wide w, the receptive o. Womb. In our crescent the children for all their size seem to come out of you toward me, wet fingers and eyes, tinted bronze. Three children, five persons, seven years. Seven years since I wed wide warm woman, white-thighed. Wooed and wed. Wife. A knife of a word that for all its final bite did not end the wooing. To my wonderment.

We eat meat, meat I wrestled warm from the raw hands of

79

the hamburger girl in the diner a mile away, a ferocious place, slick with savagery, wild with chrome; young predators snarling dirty jokes menaced me, old men reached for me with coffee-warmed paws; I wielded my wallet, and won my way back. The fat brown bag of buns was warm beside me in the cold car; the smaller bag holding the two tiny cartons of French-fries emitted an even more urgent heat. Back through the black winter air to the fire, the intimate cave, where halloos and hurrahs greeted me, the deer, mouth agape and its cotton throat gushing, stretched dead across my shoulders. And now you, beside the white O of the plate upon which the children discarded with squeals of disgust the rings of translucent onion that came squeezed into the hamburgers— you push your toes an inch closer to the blaze, and the ashy white of the inside of your deep thigh is lazily laid bare, and the eternally elastic garter snaps smackwarm against my hidden heart.

Who would have thought, wide wife, back there in the white tremble of the ceremony, (in the corner of my eye I held, despite the distracting hail of ominous vows, the vibration of the cluster of stephanotis clutched against your waist), that seven years would bring us no distance, through all those warm beds, to the same trembling point, of beginning? The cells change every seven years and down in the atom, apparently, there is a strange discontinuity; as if God wills the universe anew every instant. (Ah God, dear God, tall friend of my childhood, I will never forget you, though they say dreadful things. They say rose windows in cathedrals are vaginal symbols.) Your legs, exposed as fully as by a bathing suit, yearn deeper into the amber wash of heat. Well: begin. A green jet of flame spits out sideways from a pocket of resin in a log, crying, and the orange shadows on the ceiling sway with fresh life. Begin.

"Remember, on our honeymoon, how the top of the kerosene heater made a great big rose window on the ceiling?"

"Vnn." Your chin goes to your knees, your shins draw in, all is retracted. Not much to remember, perhaps, for you; blood badly spilled, clumsiness of all sorts. "It was cold for June."

"Mommy, what was cold? What did you say?" the girl asks, enunciating angrily, determined not to let language slip on her tongue and tumble her so that we laugh.

"A house where Daddy and I stayed one time."

"I don't like dat," the boy says, and throws a half bun painted with chartreuse mustard onto the floor.

You pick it up and with beautiful sombre musing ask, "Isn't that funny? Did any of the others have mustard on them?"

"I *hate* dat," the boy insists; he is two. Language is to him thick vague handles swirling by; he grabs what he can.

"Here. He can have mine. Give me his." I pass my hamburger over, you take it, he takes it from you, there is nowhere a ripple of gratitude. There is no more praise of my heroism in fetching Sunday supper, saving you labor. Cunning, you sense, and sense that I sense your knowledge, that I had hoped to hoard your energy toward a more ecstatic spending. We sense everything between us, every ripple, existent and nonexistent; it is tiring. Courting a wife takes tenfold the strength of winning an ignorant girl. The fire shifts, shattering fragments of newspaper that carry in lighter gray the ghost of the ink of their message. You huddle your legs and bring the skirt back over them. With a sizzling noise like the sighs of the exhausted logs, the baby sucks the last from his bottle, drops it to the floor with its distasteful hoax of vacant suds, and begins to cry. His egotist's mouth opens; the delicate membrane of his satisfaction tears. You pick him up and stand. You love the baby more than me.

Who would have thought, blood once spilled, that no barrier would be broken, that you would be each time healed into a virgin again? Tall, fair, obscure, remote, and courteous.

We put the children to bed, one by one, in reverse order of birth. I am limitlessly patient, paternal, good. Yet you know. We watch the paper bags and cartons ignite on the breathing pillow of embers, read, watch television, eat crackers, it does not matter. Eleven comes. For a tingling moment you stand on the bedroom rug in your underpants, untangling your nightie; oh, fat white sweet fat fatness. In bed you read. About Richard Nixon. He fascinates you; you hate him. You know how he defeated Jerry Voorhis, martyred Mrs. Douglas, how he played poker in the Navy despite being a Quaker, every fiendish trick, every low adaptation. Oh my Lord. Let's let the poor man go to bed. We're none of us perfect. "Hey let's turn out the light."

"Wait. He's just about to get Hiss convicted. It's very strange. It says he acted honorably."

"I'm sure he did." I reach for the switch.

"No. Wait. Just till I finish this chapter. I'm sure there'll be something at the end."

"Honey, Hiss was guilty. We're all guilty. Conceived in concupiscence, we die unrepentant." Once my ornate words wooed you.

I lie against your filmy convex back. You read sideways, a sleepy trick. I see the page through the fringe of your hair, sharp and white as a wedge of crystal. Suddenly it slips. The book has slipped from your hand. You are asleep. Oh cunning trick, cunning. In the darkness I consider. Cunning. The headlights of cars accidentally slide fanning slits of light around our walls and ceiling. The great rose window was projected upward through the petal-shaped perforations in the top of the black kerosene stove, which we stood in the center of the floor. As the flame on the circular wick flickered, the wide soft star of interlocked penumbrae moved and waved as if it were printed on a silk cloth being gently tugged or slowly blown. Its color soft blurred blood. We pay dear in blood for our peaceful homes.

In the morning, to my relief, you are ugly. Monday's wan breakfast light bleaches you blotchily, drains the goodness from your thickness, makes the bathrobe a limp stained tube flapping disconsolately, exposing sallow décolletage. The skin between your breasts a sad yellow. I feast with the coffee on your drabness. Every wrinkle and sickly tint a relief and a revenge. The children yammer. The toaster sticks. Seven years have worn this woman.

The man, he arrows off to work, jousting for right-of-way, veering on the thin hard edge of the legal speed limit. Out of domestic muddle, softness, pallor, flaccidity: into the city. Stone is his province. The winning of coin. The maneuvering of abstractions. Making heartless things run. Oh the inanimate, adamant joys of job!

I return with my head enmeshed in a machine. A technicality it would take weeks to explain to you snags my brain; I fiddle with phrases and numbers all the blind evening. You serve me supper as a waitress—as less than a waitress, for I have known you. The children touch me timidly, as they would a steep girder bolted into a framework whose height they don't understand. They drift into sleep securely. We survive their passing in calm parallelity. My thoughts rework in chronic right angles the same snagging circuits on the same professional grid. You rustle the book about Nixon;

vanish upstairs into the plumbing; the bathtub pipes cry. In my head I seem to have found the stuck switch at last: I push at it; it jams; I push; it is jammed. I grow dizzy, churning with cigarettes. I circle the room aimlessly.

So I am taken by surprise at a turning when at the meaningful hour of ten you come with a kiss of toothpaste to me moist and girlish and quick; the momentous moral of this story being, An expected gift is not worth giving.

Pigeon Feathers

WHEN THEY MOVED TO FIRETOWN, things were upset, displaced, rearranged. A red cane-back sofa that had been the chief piece in the living room at Olinger was here banished, too big for the narrow country parlor, to the barn, and shrouded under a tarpaulin. Never again would David lie on its length all afternoon eating raisins and reading mystery novels and science fiction and P. G. Wodehouse. The blue wing chair that had stood for years in the ghostly, immaculate guest bedroom, gazing through the windows curtained with dotted swiss toward the telephone wires and horse-chestnut trees and opposite houses, was here established importantly in front of the smutty little fireplace that supplied, in those first cold April days, their only heat. As a child, David had been afraid of the guest bedroom—it was there that he, lying sick with the measles, had seen a black rod the size of a yard-stick jog along at a slight slant beside the edge of the bed and vanish when he screamed—and it was disquieting to have one of the elements of its haunted atmosphere basking by the fire, in the center of the family, growing sooty with use. The books that at home had gathered dust in the case beside the piano were here hastily stacked, all out of order, in the shelves that the carpenters had built along one wall below the deep-silled windows. David, at fourteen, had been more moved than a mover; like the furniture, he had to find a new place, and on the Saturday of the second week he tried to work off some of his disorientation by arranging the books.

It was a collection obscurely depressing to him, mostly books his mother had acquired when she was young: college anthologies of Greek plays and Romantic poetry, Will Durant's *Story of Philosophy*, a soft-leather set of Shakespeare with string bookmarks sewed to the bindings, *Green Mansions* boxed and illustrated with woodcuts, *I, the Tiger*, by Manuel

Komroff, novels by names like Galsworthy and Ellen Glasgow and Irvin S. Cobb and Sinclair Lewis and "Elizabeth." The odor of faded taste made him feel the ominous gap between himself and his parents, the insulting gulf of time that existed before he was born. Suddenly he was tempted to dip into this time. From the heaps of books piled around him on the worn old floorboards, he picked up Volume II of a four-volume set of *The Outline of History,* by H. G. Wells. Once David had read *The Time Machine* in an anthology; this gave him a small grip on the author. The book's red binding had faded to orange-pink on the spine. When he lifted the cover, there was a sweetish, attic-like smell, and his mother's maiden name written in unfamiliar handwriting on the flyleaf—an upright, bold, yet careful signature, bearing a faint relation to the quick scrunched backslant that flowed with marvellous consistency across her shopping lists and budget accounts and Christmas cards to college friends from this same, vaguely menacing long ago.

He leafed through, pausing at drawings, done in an old-fashioned stippled style, of bas-reliefs, masks, Romans without pupils in their eyes, articles of ancient costume, fragments of pottery found in unearthed homes. He knew it would be interesting in a magazine, sandwiched between ads and jokes, but in this undiluted form history was somehow sour. The print was determinedly legible, and smug, like a lesson book. As he bent over the pages, yellow at the edges, they seemed rectangles of dusty glass through which he looked down into unreal and irrelevant worlds. He could see things sluggishly move, and an unpleasant fullness came into his throat. His mother and grandmother fussed in the kitchen; the puppy, which they had just acquired, for "protection in the country," was cowering, with a sporadic panicked scrabble of claws, under the dining table that in their old home had been reserved for special days but that here was used for every meal.

Then, before he could halt his eyes, David slipped into Wells's account of Jesus. He had been an obscure political agitator, a kind of hobo, in a minor colony of the Roman Empire. By an accident impossible to reconstruct, he (the small *h* horrified David) survived his own crucifixion and presumably died a few weeks later. A religion was founded on the freakish incident. The credulous imagination of the times retrospectively assigned miracles and supernatural pretensions to Jesus; a myth grew, and then a church, whose theology at most points was in direct contradiction of the simple, rather communistic teachings of the Galilean.

It was as if a stone that for weeks and even years had been gathering weight in the web of David's nerves snapped them and plunged through the page and a hundred layers of paper underneath. These fantastic falsehoods—plainly untrue; churches stood everywhere, the entire nation was founded "under God"—did not at first frighten him; it was the fact that they had not been permitted to exist in an actual human brain. This was the initial impact—that at a definite spot in time and space a brain black with the denial of Christ's divinity had been suffered to exist; that the universe had not spit out this ball of tar but allowed it to continue in its blasphemy, to grow old, win honors, wear a hat, write books that, if true, collapsed everything into a jumble of horror. The world outside the deep-silled windows—a rutted lawn, a whitewashed barn, a walnut tree frothy with fresh green—seemed a haven from which he was forever sealed off. Hot washrags seemed pressed against his cheeks.

He read the account again. He tried to supply out of his ignorance objections that would defeat the complacent march of these black words, and found none. Survivals and misunderstandings more far-fetched were reported daily in the papers. But none of them caused churches to be built in every town. He tried to work backwards through the churches, from their h⸱   high fronts through their shabby, ill-attended interiors back into the events at Jerusalem, and felt himself surrounded by shifting gray shadows, centuries of history, where he knew nothing. The thread dissolved in his hands. Had Christ ever come to him, David Kern, and said, "Here. Feel the wound in My side?" No; but prayers had been answered. What prayers? He had prayed that Rudy Mohn, whom he had purposely tripped so he cracked his head on their radiator, not die, and he had not died. But for all the blood, it was just a cut; Rudy came back the same day, wearing a bandage and repeating the same teasing words. He could never have died. Again, David had prayed for two separate war-effort posters he had sent away for to arrive tomorrow, and though they did not, they did arrive, some days later, together, popping through the clacking letter slot like a rebuke from God's mouth: *I answer your prayers in My way, in My time.* After that, he had made his prayers less definite, less susceptible of being twisted into a scolding. But what a tiny, ridiculous coincidence this was, after all, to throw into battle against

H. G. Wells's engines of knowledge! Indeed, it proved the enemy's point: Hope bases vast premises on foolish accidents, and reads a word where in fact only a scribble exists.

His father came home. Though Saturday was a free day for him, he had been working. He taught school in Olinger and spent all his days performing, with a curious air of panic, needless errands. Also, a city boy by birth, he was frightened of the farm and seized any excuse to get away. The farm had been David's mother's birthplace; it had been her idea to buy it back. With an ingenuity and persistence unparalleled in her life, she had gained that end, and moved them all here—her son, her husband, her mother. Granmom, in her prime, had worked these fields alongside her husband, but now she dabbled around the kitchen futilely, her hands waggling with Parkinson's disease. She was always in the way. Strange, out in the country, amid eighty acres, they were crowded together. His father expressed his feelings of discomfort by conducting with Mother an endless argument about organic farming. All through dusk, all through supper, it rattled on.

"Elsie, I *know,* I know from my education, the earth is nothing but chemicals. It's the only damn thing I got out of four years of college, so don't tell me it's not true."

"George, if you'd just walk out on the farm you'd know it's not true. The land has a *soul.*"

"Soil, has, no, soul," he said, enunciating stiffly, as if to a very stupid class. To David he said, "You can't argue with a femme. Your mother's a real femme. That's why I married her, and now I'm suffering for it."

"*This* soil has no soul," she said, "because it's been killed with superphosphate. It's been burned bare by Boyer's tenant farmers." Boyer was the rich man they had bought the farm from. "It used to have a soul, didn't it, Mother? When you and Pop farmed it?"

"Ach, yes; I guess." Granmom was trying to bring a forkful of food to her mouth with her less severely afflicted hand. In her anxiety she brought the other hand up from her lap. The crippled fingers, dull red in the orange light of the kerosene lamp in the center of the table, were welded by paralysis into one knobbed hook.

"Only human indi-vidu-als have souls," his father went on, in the same mincing, lifeless voice. "Because the Bible tells us so." Done eating, he crossed his legs and dug into his ear with a match miserably; to get at the thing inside his head he tucked in his chin, and his voice came out low-pitched at David. "When God made your mother, He made a real femme."

"George, don't you read the papers? Don't you know that between the chemical fertilizers and the bug sprays we'll all be dead in ten years? Heart attacks are killing every man in the country over forty-five."

He sighed wearily; the yellow skin of his eyelids wrinkled as he hurt himself with the match. "There's no connection," he stated, spacing his words with pained patience, "between the heart - and chemical fertilizers. It's alcohol that's doing it. Alcohol and milk. There is too much - cholesterol - in the tissues of the American heart. Don't tell me about chemistry, Elsie; I majored in the damn stuff for four years."

"Yes and I majored in Greek and I'm not a penny wiser. Mother, put your waggler *away!*" The old woman started, and the food dropped from her fork. For some reason, the sight of her bad hand at the table cruelly irritated her daughter. Granmom's eyes, worn bits of crazed crystal embedded in watery milk, widened behind her cockeyed spectacles. Circles of silver as fine as thread, they clung to the red notches they had carved over the years into her little white beak. In the orange flicker of the kerosene lamp her dazed misery seemed infernal. David's mother began, without noise, to cry. His father did not seem to have eyes at all; just jaundiced sockets of wrinkled skin. The steam of food clouded the scene. It was horrible but the horror was particular and familiar, and distracted David from the formless dread that worked, sticky and sore, within him, like a too large wound trying to heal.

He had to go to the bathroom, and took a flashlight down through the wet grass to the outhouse. For once, his fear of spiders there felt trivial. He set the flashlight, burning, beside him, and an insect alighted on its lens, a tiny insect, a mosquito or flea, made so fine that the weak light projected its X-ray onto the wall boards; the faint rim of its wings, the blurred strokes, magnified, of its long hinged legs, the dark cone at the heart of its anatomy. The tremor must be its heart beating. Without warning, David was visited by an exact vision of death: a long hole in the ground, no wider than your body, down which you are drawn while the white faces above recede. You try to reach them but your arms are pinned. Shovels pour dirt into your face. There you will be forever, in an upright position(blind and silent, and in time no one will remember you, and you will never be called. As strata of rock shift, your fingers elongate, and your teeth are distended sideways in a great underground grimace indistinguishable from a strip of chalk. And the earth tumbles on, and the sun expires, and unaltering darkness reigns where once there were stars.

Sweat broke out on his back. His mind seemed to rebound off a solidness. Such extinction was not another threat, a graver sort of danger, a kind of pain; it was qualitatively different. It was not even a conception that could be voluntarily pictured; it entered him from outside. His protesting nerves swarmed on its surface like lichen on a meteor. The skin of his chest was soaked with the effort of rejection. At the same time that the fear was dense and internal, it was dense and all around him; a tide of clay had swept up to the stars; space was crushed into a mass. When he stood up, automatically hunching his shoulders to keep his head away from the spider webs, it was with a numb sense of being cramped between two huge volumes of rigidity. That he had even this small freedom to move surprised him. In the narrow shelter of that rank shack, adjusting his pants, he felt—his first spark of comfort—too small to be crushed.

But in the open, as the beam of the flashlight skidded with frightened quickness across the remote surfaces of the barn and the grape arbor and the giant pine that stood by the path to the woods, the terror descended. He raced up through the clinging grass pursued, not by one of the wild animals the woods might hold, or one of the goblins his superstitious grandmother had communicated to his childhood, but by spectres out of science fiction, where gigantic cinder moons fill half the turquoise sky. As David ran, a gray planet rolled inches behind his neck. If he looked back, he would be buried. And in the momentum of his terror, hideous possibilities— the dilation of the sun, the triumph of the insects, the crabs on the shore in *The Time Machine*—wheeled out of the vacuum of make-believe and added their weight to his impending oblivion.

He wrenched the door open; the lamps within the house flared. The wicks burning here and there seemed to mirror one another. His mother was washing the dishes in a little pan of heated pump-water; Granmom fluttered near her elbow apprehensive. In the living room—the downstairs of the little square house was two long rooms—his father sat in front of the black fire place restlessly folding and unfolding a newspaper as he sustained his half of the argument. "Nitrogen, phosphorus, potash: these are the three replaceable constituents of the soil. One crop of corn carries away hundreds of pounds of"—he dropped the paper into his lap and ticked them off on three fingers—"nitrogen, phosphorus, potash."

"Boyer didn't grow corn."

"*Any* crop, Elsie. The human animal—"

"You're killing the *earth*worms, George!"

"The human animal, after thousands and *thous*ands of years, learned methods whereby the chemical balance of the soil may be maintained. Don't carry me back to the Dark Ages."

"When we moved to Olinger the ground in the garden was like slate. Just one summer of my cousin's chicken dung and the earthworms came back."

"I'm sure the Dark Ages were a fine place to the poor devils born in them, but I don't want to go there. They give me the creeps." Daddy stared into the cold pit of the fireplace and clung to the rolled newspaper in his lap as if it alone were keeping him from slipping backwards and down, down.

Mother came into the doorway brandishing a fistful of wet forks. "And thanks to your DDT there soon won't be a bee left in the country. When I was a girl here you could eat a peach without washing it."

"It's primitive, Elsie. It's Dark Age stuff."

"Oh what do *you* know about the Dark Ages?"

"I know I don't want to go back to them."

David took from the shelf, where he had placed it this afternoon, the great unabridged Webster's Dictionary that his grandfather had owned. He turned the big thin pages, floppy as cloth, to the entry he wanted, and read

soul . . . 1. An entity conceived as the essence, substance, animating principle, or actuating cause of life, or of the individual life, esp. of life manifested in psychical activities; the vehicle of individual existence, separate in nature from the body and usually held to be separable in existence.

The definition went on, into Greek and Egyptian conceptions, but David stopped short on the treacherous edge of antiquity. He needed to read no further. The careful overlapping words shingled a temporary shelter for him. "Usually held to be separable in existence"—what could be fairer, more judicious, surer?

His father was saying, "The modern farmer can't go around sweeping up after his cows. The poor devil has thousands and *thou*sands of acres on his hands. Your modern farmer uses a scientifically-arrived-at mixture, like five-ten-five, or six-twelve-six, or *three*-twelve-six, and spreads it on with this wonderful modern machinery which of course we can't afford. Your modern farmer can't *afford* medieval methods."

Mother was quiet in the kitchen; her silence radiated waves of anger.

"No now Elsie; don't play the femme with me. Let's discuss this calmly like two rational twentieth-century people. Your organic farming nuts aren't attacking five-ten-five; they're attacking the chemical fertilizer crooks. The monster firms."

A cup clinked in the kitchen. Mother's anger touched David's face; his cheeks burned guiltily. Just by being in the living room he was associated with his father. She appeared in the doorway with red hands and tears in her eyes, and said to the two of them, "I knew you didn't want to come here but I didn't know you'd torment me like this. You talked Pop into his grave and now you'll kill me. Go ahead, George, more power to you; at least I'll be buried in good ground." She tried to turn and met an obstacle and screamed, "Mother, stop hanging on my *back!* Why don't you go to *bed?*"

"Let's all go to bed," David's father said, rising from the blue wing chair and slapping his thigh with a newspaper. "This reminds me of death." It was a phrase of his that David had heard so often he never considered its sense.

Upstairs, he seemed to be lifted above his fears. The sheets on his bed were clean. Granmom had ironed them with a pair of flatirons saved from the Olinger attic; she plucked them hot off the stove alternately, with a wooden handle called a goose. It was a wonder, to see how she managed. In the next room, his parents grunted peaceably; they seemed to take their quarrels less seriously than he did. They made comfortable scratching noises as they carried a little lamp back and forth. Their door was open a crack, so he saw the light shift and swing. Surely there would be, in the last few minutes, in the last second, a crack of light, showing the door from the dark room to another, full of light. Thinking of it this vividly frightened him. His own dying, in a specific bed in a specific room, specific walls mottled with wallpaper, the dry whistle of his breathing, the murmuring doctors, the nervous relatives going in and out, but for him no way out but down into the funnel. *Never touch a doorknob again.* A whisper, and his parents' light was blown out. David prayed to be reassured. Though the experiment frightened him, he lifted his hands high into the darkness above his face and begged Christ to touch them. Not hard or long: the faintest, quickest grip would be final for a lifetime. His hands waited in the air, itself a substance, which seemed to move through his fingers; or was it the pressure of his pulse? He returned his hands to beneath the covers uncertain if they had been touched or not. For would not Christ's touch *be* infinitely gentle?

Through all the eddies of its aftermath, David clung to this thought about his revelation of extinction: that there, in the outhouse, he had struck a solidness qualitatively different, a rock of horror firm enough to support any height of construction. All he needed was a little help; a word, a gesture, a nod of certainty, and he would be sealed in, safe. The assurance from the dictionary had melted in the night. Today was Sunday, a hot fair day. Across a mile of clear air the church bells called, *Celebrate, celebrate*. Only Daddy went. He put on a coat over his rolled-up shirtsleeves and got into the little old black Plymouth parked by the barn and went off, with the same pained hurried grimness of all his actions. His churning wheels, as he shifted too hastily into second, raised plumes of red dust on the dirt road. Mother walked to the far field, to see what bushes needed cutting. David, though he usually preferred to stay in the house, went with her. The puppy followed at a distance, whining as it picked its way through the stubble but floundering off timidly if one of them went back to pick it up and carry it. When they reached the crest of the far field, his mother asked, "David, what's troubling you?"

"Nothing. Why?"

She looked at him sharply. The greening woods crosshatched the space beyond her half-gray hair. Then she showed him her profile, and gestured toward the house, which they had left a half-mile behind them. "See how it sits in the land? They don't know how to build with the land any more. Pop always said the foundations were set with the compass. We must try to get a compass and see. It's supposed to face due south; but south feels a little more *that* way to me." From the side, as she said these things, she seemed handsome and young. The smooth sweep of her hair over her ear seemed white with a purity and calm that made her feel foreign to him. He had never regarded his parents as consolers of his troubles; from the beginning they had seemed to have more troubles than he. Their confusion had flattered him into an illusion of strength; so now on this high clear ridge he jealously guarded the menace all around them, blowing like a breeze on his fingertips, the possibility of all this wide scenery sinking into darkness. The strange fact that though she came to look at the brush she carried no clippers, for she had a fixed prejudice against working on Sundays, was the only consolation he allowed her to offer.

As they walked back, the puppy whimpering after them, the rising dust behind a distant line of trees announced that Daddy was speeding home from church. When they reached the house he was there. He had brought back the Sunday paper and the vehement remark, "Dobson's too intelligent for these farmers. They just sit there with their mouths open and don't hear a thing the poor devil's saying."

"What makes you think farmers are unintelligent? This country was made by farmers. George Washington was a farmer."

"They are, Elsie. They are unintelligent. George Washington's dead. In this day and age only the misfits stay on the farm. The lame, the halt, the blind. The morons with one arm. Human garbage. They remind me of death, sitting there with their mouths open."

"My *father* was a farmer."

"He was a frustrated man, Elsie. He never knew what hit him. The poor devil meant so well, and he never knew which end was up. Your mother'll bear me out. Isn't that right, Mom? Pop never knew what hit him?"

"Ach, I guess not," the old woman quavered, and the ambiguity for the moment silenced both sides.

David hid in the funny papers and sports section until one-thirty. At two, the catechetical class met at the Firetown church. He had transferred from the catechetical class of the Lutheran church in Olinger, a humiliating comedown. In Olinger they met on Wednesday nights, spiffy and spruce, in the atmosphere of a dance. Afterwards, blessed by the brick-faced minister from whose lips the word "Christ" fell like a burning stone, the more daring of them went with their Bibles to a luncheonette and smoked. Here in Firetown, the girls were dull white cows and the boys narrow-faced brown goats in old men's suits, herded on Sunday afternoons into a threadbare church basement that smelled of stale hay. Because his father had taken the car on one of his endless errands to Olinger, David walked, grateful for the open air and the silence. The catechetical class embarrassed him, but today he placed hope in it, as the source of the nod, the gesture, that was all he needed.

Reverend Dobson was a delicate young man with great dark eyes and small white shapely hands that flickered like protesting doves when he preached; he seemed a bit misplaced in the Lutheran ministry. This was his first call. It was a split parish; he served another rural church twelve miles away. His iridescent green Ford, new six months ago, was spattered to the windows with red mud and rattled from bouncing on the rude back roads, where he frequently got lost, to the malicious satisfaction of many. But David's mother liked him, and, more pertinent to his success, the Haiers, the sleek family of feed merchants and innkeepers and tractor salesmen who dominated the Firetown church, liked him. David liked him, and felt liked in turn; sometimes in class, after some special stupidity, Dobson directed toward him out of those wide black eyes a mild look of disbelief, a look that, though flattering, was also delicately disquieting.

Catechetical instruction consisted of reading aloud from a work booklet answers to problems prepared during the week, problems like, "I am the _____, the _____, and the _____, saith the Lord." Then there was a question period in which no one ever asked any questions. Today's theme was the last third of the Apostles' Creed. When the time came for questions, David blushed and asked, "About the Resurrection of the Body—are we conscious between the time when we die and the Day of Judgment?"

Dobson blinked, and his fine little mouth pursed, suggesting that David was making difficult things more difficult. The faces of the other students went blank, as if an indiscretion had been committed.

"No, I suppose not," Reverend Dobson said.

"Well, where is our soul, then, in this gap?"

The sense grew, in the class, of a naughtiness occurring. Dobson's shy eyes watered, as if he were straining to keep up the formality of attention, and one of the girls, the fattest, simpered toward her twin, who was a little less fat. Their chairs were arranged in a rough circle. The current running around the circle panicked David. Did everybody know something he didn't know?

"I suppose you could say our souls are asleep," Dobson said.

"And then they wake up, and there is the earth like it

always is, and all the people who have ever lived? Where will Heaven be?"

Anita Haier giggled. Dobson gazed at David intently, but with an awkward, puzzled flicker of forgiveness, as if there existed a secret between them that David was violating. But David knew of no secret. All he wanted was to hear Dobson repeat the words he said every Sunday morning. This he would not do. As if these words were unworthy of the conversational voice.

"David, you might think of Heaven this way: as the way the goodness Abraham Lincoln did lives after him."

"But is Lincoln conscious of it living on?" He blushed no longer with embarrassment but in anger; he had walked here in good faith and was being made a fool.

"Is he conscious now? I would have to say no; but I don't think it matters." His voice had a coward's firmness; he was hostile now.

"You don't."

"Not in the eyes of God, no." The unction, the stunning impudence, of this reply sprang tears of outrage in David's eyes. He bowed them to his book, where short words like Duty, Love, Obey, Honor, were stacked in the form of a cross.

"Were there any other questions, David?" Dobson asked with renewed gentleness. The others were rustling, collecting their books.

"No." He made his voice firm, though he could not bring up his eyes.

"Did I answer your question fully enough?"

"Yes."

In the minister's silence the shame that should have been his crept over David: the burden and fever of being a fraud were placed upon *him*, who was innocent, and it seemed, he knew, a confession of this guilt that on the way out he was unable to face Dobson's stirred gaze, though he felt it probing the side of his head.

Anita Haier's father gave him a ride down the highway as far as the dirt road. David said he wanted to walk the rest, and figured that his offer was accepted because Mr. Haier did not want to dirty his bright blue Buick with dust. This was all right; everything was all right, as long as it was clear. His indignation at being betrayed, at seeing Christianity betrayed, had hardened him. The straight dirt road reflected his hardness. Pink stones thrust up through its packed surface. The April sun beat down from the center of the afternoon half of the sky; already it had some of summer's heat. Already the fringes of weeds at the edges of the road were bedraggled with dust. From the reviving grass and scuff of the fields he walked between, insects were sending up a monotonous, automatic chant. In the distance a tiny figure in his father's coat was walking along the edge of the woods. His mother. He wondered what joy she found in such walks; to him the brown stretches of slowly rising and falling land expressed only a huge exhaustion.

Flushed with fresh air and happiness, she returned from her walk earlier than he had expected, and surprised him at his grandfather's Bible. It was a stumpy black book, the boards worn thin where the old man's fingers had held them; the spine hung by one weak hinge of fabric. David had been looking for the passage where Jesus says to the one thief on the cross, "Today shalt though be with me in paradise." He had never tried reading the Bible for himself before. What was so embarrassing about being caught at it, was that he detested the apparatus of piety. Fusty churches, creaking hymns, ugly Sunday-school teachers and their stupid leaflets— he hated everything about them but the promise they held out, a promise that in the most perverse way, as if the homeliest crone in the kingdom were given the Prince's hand, made every good and real thing, ball games and jokes and pert-breasted girls, possible. He couldn't explain this to his mother. There was no time. Her solicitude was upon him.

"David, what are you doing?"

"Nothing."

"What are you doing at Grandpop's Bible?"

"Trying to read it. This is supposed to be a Christian country, isn't it?"

She sat down on the green sofa, which used to be in the sun parlor at Olinger, under the fancy mirror. A little smile still lingered on her face from the walk. "David, I wish you'd talk to me."

"What about?"

"About whatever it is that's troubling you. Your father and I have both noticed it."

"I asked Reverend Dobson about Heaven and he said it was like Abraham Lincoln's goodness living after him."

He waited for the shock to strike her. "Yes?" she said, expecting more.

"That's all."

"And why didn't you like it?"

"Well; don't you see? It amounts to saying there isn't any Heaven at all."

"I don't see that it amounts to that. What do you want Heaven to be?"

"Well, I don't know. I want it to be *some*thing. I thought he'd tell me what it was. I thought that was his job." He was becoming angry, sensing her surprise at him. She had assumed that Heaven had faded from his head years ago. She had imagined that he had already entered, in the secrecy of silence, the conspiracy that she now knew to be all around him.

"David," she asked gently, "don't you ever want to rest?"

"No. Not forever."

"David, you're so young. When you get older, you'll feel differently."

"Grandpa didn't. Look how tattered this book is."

"I never understood your grandfather."

"Well I don't understand ministers who say it's like Lincoln's goodness going on and on. Suppose you're not Lincoln?"

"I think Reverend Dobson made a mistake. You must try to forgive him."

"It's not a *question* of his making a mistake! It's a question of dying and never moving or seeing or hearing anything ever again."

"But"—in exasperation—"darling, it's so *greedy* of you to want more. When God has given us this wonderful April day, and given us this farm, and you have your whole life ahead of you—"

"You think, then, that there is God?"

"Of course I do"—with deep relief, that smoothed her features into a reposeful oval. He had risen and was standing too near her for his comfort. He was afraid she would reach out and touch him.

"He made everything? You feel that?"

"Yes."

"Then who made Him?"

"Why, Man. Man." The happiness of this answer lit up her face radiantly, until she saw his gesture of disgust. She was so simple, so illogical; such a femme.

"Well that amounts to saying there is none."

Her hand reached for his wrist but he backed away. "David, it's a mystery. A miracle. It's a miracle more beautiful than any Reverend Dobson could have told you about. You don't say houses don't exist because Man made them."

"No. God has to be different."

"But, David, you have the *evidence*. Look out the window at the sun; at the fields."

"Mother, good grief. Don't you see"—he rasped away the roughness in his throat—"if when we die there's nothing, all your sun and fields and what not are all, ah, *horror*? It's just an ocean of horror."

"But David, it's not. It's so clearly not that." And she made an urgent opening gesture with her hands that expressed, with its suggestion of a willingness to receive his helplessness, all her grace, her gentleness, her love of beauty, gathered into a passive intensity that made him intensely hate her. He would not be wooed away from the truth. *I am the Way, the Truth* . . .

"No," he told her. "Just let me alone."

He found his tennis ball behind the piano and went outside to throw it against the side of the house. There was a patch high up where the brown stucco that had been laid over the sandstone masonry was crumbling away; he kept trying with the tennis ball to chip more pieces off. Superimposed upon his deep ache was a smaller but more immediate worry; that he had hurt his mother. He heard his father's car rattling on the straightaway, and went into the house, to make peace before he arrived. To his relief, she was not giving off the stifling damp heat of her anger, but instead was cool, decisive, maternal. She handed him an old green book, her college text of Plato.

"I want you to read the Parable of the Cave," she said.

"All right," he said, though he knew it would do no good. Some story by a dead Greek just vague enough to please her. "Don't worry about it, Mother."

"I *am* worried. Honestly, David, I'm sure there will be something for us. As you get older, these things seem to matter a great deal less."

"That may be. It's a dismal thought, though."

His father bumped at the door. The locks and jambs stuck here. But before Granmom could totter to the latch and let him in, he had knocked it open. He had been in Olinger dithering with track meet tickets. Although Mother usually kept her talks with David a confidence, a treasure between them, she called instantly, "George, David is worried about death!"

He came to the doorway of the living room, his shirt pocket bristling with pencils, holding in one hand a pint box of melting ice cream and in the other the knife with which he was about to divide it into four sections, their Sunday treat. "Is the kid worried about death? Don't give it a thought, David. I'll be lucky if I live till tomorrow, and I'm not worried. If they'd taken a buckshot gun and shot me in the cradle I'd be better off. The *world*'d be better off. Hell, I think death is a wonderful thing. I look forward to it. Get the garbage out of the way. If I had the man here who invented death, I'd pin a medal on him."

"Hush, George. You'll frighten the child worse than he is."

This was not true; he never frightened David. There was no harm in his father, no harm at all. Indeed, in the man's steep self-disgust the boy felt a kind of ally. A distant ally. He saw his position with a certain strategic coldness. Nowhere in the world of other people would he find the hint, the nod, he needed to begin to build his fortress against death. They none of them believed. He was alone. In that deep hole.

In the months that followed, his position changed little. School was some comfort. All those sexy, perfumed people, wisecracking, chewing gum, all of them doomed to die, and none of them noticing. In their company David felt that they would carry him along into the bright, cheap paradise reserved for them. In any crowd, the fear ebbed a little; he had reasoned that somewhere in the world there must exist a few people who believed what was necessary, and the larger the crowd, the greater the chance that he was near such a soul, within calling distance, if only he was not too ignorant, too ill-equipped, to spot him. The sight of clergymen cheered him; whatever they themselves thought, their collars were still a sign that somewhere, at sometime, someone had recognized that we cannot, *cannot*, submit to death. The sermon topics posted outside churches, the flip, hurried pieties of disc jockeys, the cartoons in magazines showing angels or devils —on such scraps he kept alive the possibility of hope.

For the rest, he tried to drown his hopelessness in clatter and jostle. The pinball machine at the luncheonette was a merciful distraction; as he bent over its buzzing, flashing board of flippers and cushions, the weight and constriction in his chest lightened and loosened. He was grateful for all the time his father wasted in Olinger. Every delay postponed the moment when they must ride together down the dirt road into the heart of the dark farmland, where the only light was the kerosene lamp waiting on the dining-room table, a light that drowned their food in shadow and made it sinister.

He lost his appetite for reading. He was afraid of being ambushed again. In mystery novels people died like dolls being discarded; in science fiction enormities of space and time conspired to crush the humans; and even in P. G. Wodehouse he felt a hollowness, a turning away from reality that was implicitly bitter, and became explicit in the comic figures of futile clergymen. All gaiety seemed minced out on the skin of a void. All quiet hours seemed invitations to dread.

Even on weekends, he and his father contrived to escape the farm; and when, some Saturdays, they did stay home, it was to do something destructive—tear down an old henhouse or set huge brush fires that threatened, while Mother shouted and flapped her arms, to spread to the woods. Whenever his father worked, it was with rapt violence; when he chopped kindling, fragments of the old henhouse boards flew like shrapnel and the ax-head was always within a quarter of an inch of flying off the handle. He was exhilarating to watch, sweating and swearing and sucking bits of saliva back into his lips.

School stopped. His father took the car in the opposite direction, to a highway construction job where he had been hired for the summer as a timekeeper, and David was stranded in the middle of acres of heat and greenery and blowing pollen and the strange, mechanical humming that lay invisibly in the weeds and alfalfa and dry orchard grass.

For his fifteenth birthday his parents gave him, with jokes about him being a hillbilly now, a Remington .22. It was somewhat like a pinball machine to take it out to the old kiln in the woods where they dumped their trash, and set up tin cans on the kiln's sandstone shoulder and shoot them off one by one. He'd take the puppy, who had grown long legs and a rich coat of reddish fur—he was part chow. Copper hated the gun but loved the boy enough to accompany him. When the flat acrid crack rang out, he would race in terrified circles that would tighten and tighten until they brought him, shivering, against David's legs. Depending upon his mood, David would shoot again or drop to his knees and comfort the dog. Giving this comfort to a degree returned comfort to him. The dog's ears, laid flat against his skull in fear, were folded so intricately, so—he groped for the concept—*surely*. Where the dull-studded collar made the fur stand up, each hair showed a root of soft white under the length, black-tipped, of the metal-color that had lent the dog its name. In his agitation Copper panted through nostrils that were elegant slits, like two healed cuts, or like the key-holes of a dainty lock of black, grained wood. His whole whorling, knotted, jointed body was a wealth of such embellishments. And in the smell of the dog's hair David seemed to descend through many finely differentiated layers of earth: mulch, soil, sand, clay, and the glittering mineral base.

But when he returned to the house, and saw the books arranged on the low shelves, fear returned. The four adamant volumes of Wells like four thin bricks, the green Plato that had puzzled him with its queer softness and tangled purity, the dead Galsworthy and "Elizabeth," Grandpa's mammoth dictionary, Grandpa's Bible, the Bible that he himself had received on becoming a member of the Firetown Lutheran Church—at the sight of these, the memory of his fear re-awakened and came around him. He had grown stiff and stupid in its embrace. His parents tried to think of ways to entertain him.

"David, I have a job for you to do," his mother said one evening at the table.

"What?"

"If you're going to take that tone perhaps we'd better not talk."

"What tone? I didn't take any tone."

"Your grandmother thinks there are too many pigeons in the barn."

"Why?" David turned to look at his grandmother, but she sat there staring at the burning lamp with her usual expression of bewilderment.

Mother shouted, "Mom, he wants to know why!"

Granmom made a jerky, irritable motion with her bad hand, as if generating the force for utterance, and said, "They foul the furniture."

"That's right," Mother said. "She's afraid for that old Olinger furniture that we'll never use. David, she's been after me for a month about those poor pigeons. She wants you to shoot them."

"I don't want to kill anything especially," David said.

Daddy said, "The kid's like you are, Elsie. He's too good for this world. Kill or be killed, that's my motto."

His mother said loudly, "Mother, he doesn't want to do it."

"Not?" The old lady's eyes distended as if in horror, and her claw descended slowly to her lap.

"Oh, I'll do it, I'll do it tomorrow," David snapped, and a pleasant crisp taste entered his mouth with the decision.

"And I had thought, when Boyer's men made the hay, it would be better if the barn doesn't look like a rookery," his mother added needlessly.

A barn, in day, is a small night. The splinters of light between the dry singles pierce the high roof like stars, and the rafters and crossbeams and built-in ladders seem, until your eyes adjust, as mysterious as the branches of a haunted forest. David entered silently, the gun in one hand. Copper whined desperately at the door, too frightened to come in with the gun yet unwilling to leave the boy. David stealthily turned, said "Go away," shut the door on the dog, and slipped the bolt across. It was a door within a door; the double door for wagons and tractors was as high and wide as the face of a house.

The smell of old straw scratched his sinuses. The red sofa, half-hidden under its white-splotched tarpaulin, seemed assimilated into this smell, sunk in it, buried. The mouths of empty bins gaped like caves. Rusty oddments of farming—coils of baling wire, some spare tines for a harrow, a handleless shovel—hung on nails driven here and there in the thick wood. He stood stock-still a minute; it took a while to separate the cooing of the pigeons from the rustling in his ears. When he had focused on the cooing, it flooded the vast interior with its throaty, bubbling outpour: there seemed no other sound. They were up behind the beams. What light there was leaked through the shingles and the dirty glass windows at the far end and the small round holes, about as big as basketballs, high on the opposite stone side walls, under the ridge of the roof.

A pigeon appeared in one of these holes, on the side toward the house. It flew in, with a battering of wings, from the outside, and waited there, silhouetted against its pinched bit of sky, preening and cooing in a throbbing, thrilled, tentative way. David tiptoed four steps to the side, rested his gun against the lowest rung of a ladder pegged between two upright beams, and lowered the gunsight into the bird's tiny, jauntily cocked head. The slap of the report seemed to come off the stone wall behind him, and the pigeon did not fall. Neither did it fly. Instead it stuck in the round hole, pirouetting rapidly and nodding its head as if in frantic agreement. David shot the bolt back and forth and had aimed again before the spent cartridge had stopped jingling on the boards by his feet. He eased the tip of the sight a little lower, into the bird's breast, and took care to squeeze the trigger with perfect evenness. The slow contraction of his hand abruptly sprang the bullet; for a half-second there was doubt, and then the pigeon fell like a handful of rags, skimming down the barn wall into the layer of straw that coated the floor of the mow on this side.

Now others shook loose from the rafters, and whirled in the dim air with a great blurred hurtle of feathers and noise. They would go for the hole; he fixed his sight on the little moon of blue, and when a pigeon came to it, shot him as he was walking the ten inches of stone that would have carried him into the open air. This pigeon lay down in that tunnel of stone, unable to fall either way or the other, although he was alive enough to lift one wing and cloud the light. It would sink back, and he would suddenly lift it again, the feathers flaring. His body blocked that exit. David raced to the other side of the barn's main aisle, where a similar ladder was symmetrically placed, and rested his gun on the same rung. Three birds came together to this hole; he got one, and two got through. The rest resettled in the rafters.

There was a shallow triangular space behind the cross beams supporting the roof. It was here they roosted and hid. But either the space was too small, or they were curious, for now that his eyes were at home in the dusty gloom David could see little dabs of gray popping in and out. The cooing was shriller now; its apprehensive tremolo made the whole volume of air seem liquid. He noticed one little smudge of a head that was especially persistent in peeking out; he marked the place, and fixed his gun on it, and when the head appeared again, had his finger tightened in advance on the trigger. A parcel of fluff slipped off the beam and fell the barn's height onto a canvas covering some Olinger furniture, and where its head had peeked out there was a fresh prick of light in the shingles.

Standing in the center of the floor, fully master now, disdaining to steady the barrel with anything but his arm, he killed two more that way. He felt like a beautiful avenger. Out of the shadowy ragged infinity of the vast barn roof these impudent things dared to thrust their heads, presumed to dirty its starred silence with their filthy timorous life, and he cut them off, tucked them back neatly into the silence. He had the sensation of a creator; these little smudges and flickers that he was clever to see and even cleverer to hit in the dim recesses of the rafters—out of each of them he was making a full bird. A tiny peek, probe, dab of life, when he hit it, blossomed into a dead enemy, falling with good, final weight.

The imperfection of the second pigeon he had shot, who was still lifting his wing now and then up in the round hole, nagged him. He put a new clip into the stock. Hugging the gun against his body, he climbed the ladder. The barrel sight scratched his ear; he had a sharp, garish vision, like a color slide, of shooting himself and being found tumbled on the barn floor among his prey. He locked his arm around the top rung—a fragile, gnawed rod braced between uprights—and shot into the bird's body from a flat angle. The wing folded, but the impact did not, as he had hoped, push the bird out of the hole. He fired again, and again, and still the little body, lighter than air when alive, was too heavy to budge from its high grave. From up here he could see green trees and a brown corner of the house through the hole. Clammy with the cobwebs that gathered between the rungs, he pumped a full clip of eight bullets into the stubborn shadow, with no success. He climbed down, and was struck by the silence in the barn. The remaining pigeons must have escaped out the other hole. That was all right; he was tired of it.

He stepped with his rifle into the light. His mother was coming to meet him, and it tickled him to see her shy away from the carelessly held gun. "You took a chip out of the house," she said. "What were those last shots about?"

"One of them died up in that little round hole and I was trying to shoot it down."

"Copper's hiding behind the piano and won't come out. I had to leave him."

"Well don't blame me. *I* didn't want to shoot the poor devils."

"Don't smirk. You look like your father. How many did you get?"

"Six."

She went into the barn, and he followed. She listened to the silence. Her hair was scraggly, perhaps from tussling with the dog. "I don't suppose the others will be back," she said wearily. "Indeed, I don't know why I let Mother talk me into it. Their cooing was such a comforting noise." She began to gather up the dead pigeons. Though he didn't want to touch them, David went into the mow and picked up by its tepid, horny, coral-colored feet the first bird he had killed. Its wings unfolded disconcertingly, as if the creature had been held together by threads that now were slit. It did not weigh much. He retrieved the one on the other side of the barn; his mother got the three in the middle and led the way across the road to the little southern slope of land that went down toward the foundations of the vanished tobacco shed. The ground was too steep to plant and mow; wild strawberries grew in the tangled grass. She put her burden down and said, "We'll have to bury them. The dog will go wild."

He put his two down on her three; the slick feathers let the bodies slide liquidly on one another. He asked, "Shall I get you the shovel?"

"Get it for yourself; *you* bury them. They're your kill. And be sure to make the hole deep enough so he won't dig them up." While he went to the tool shed for the shovel, she went into the house. Unlike her, she did not look up, either at the orchard to the right of her or at the meadow on her left, but instead held her head rigidly, tilted a little, as if listening to the ground.

He dug the hole, in a spot where there were no strawberry plants, before he studied the pigeons. He had never seen a bird this close before. The feathers were more wonderful than dog's hair, for each filament was shaped within the shape of the feather, and the feathers in turn were trimmed to fit a pattern that flowed without error across the bird's body. He lost himself in the geometrical tides as the feathers now broadened and stiffened to make an edge for flight, now softened and constricted to cup warmth around the mute flesh. And across the surface of the infinitely adjusted yet somehow effortless mechanics of the feathers played idle designs of color, no two alike, designs executed, it seemed, in a controlled rapture, with a joy that hung level in the air above and behind him. Yet these birds bred in the millions and were exterminated as pests. Into the fragrant open earth he dropped one broadly banded in slate shades of blue, and on top of it another, mottled all over in rhythms of lilac and gray. The next was almost wholly white, but for a salmon glaze at its throat. As he fitted the last two, still pliant, on the top, and stood up, crusty coverings were lifted from him, and with a feminine, slipping sensation along his nerves that seemed to give the air hands, he was robed in this certainty: that the God who had lavished such craft upon these worthless birds would not destroy His whole Creation by refusing to let David live forever.

Home

FIRST, the boat trip home: a downpour in Liverpool, and on
the wharf two girls (harlots?) singing "Don't Sit Under the
Apple Tree" under a single raincoat held over their heads
like a canopy, everyone else huddling under the eaves of the
warehouses, but these girls coming right down to the edge of
the concrete wharf, singing, in effect to the whole ocean liner
but more particularly to some person or persons (a pair of
sailor lovers?) under the tourist deck. And then Cobh in
golden sunlight, and an American girl from Virginia coming
out on the pilot boat in tight toreador pants and with the
Modern Library *Ulysses* ostentatiously under her arm. And
then the days of the flawless circular horizon: blackjack with
the Rhodes Scholars, and deck tennis with the Fulbrights,
and bouillon, and the waves folding under by the prow, and
the wake wandering behind them like a lime-colored highway. Robert had determined to be not disappointed by the
Statue of Liberty, to submit to her cliché, but she disappointed
him by being genuinely awesome, in the morning mist of the
harbor, with a catch in her green body as if she had just
thought to raise the torch, or at least raise it so high. The baby
in her bunting wriggled on his shoulder, and the other young
Americans crowded the rail, and he felt obstructed from
absorbing a classic effect, the queen of insignia, the trademark supreme. So it was he, prepared to condescend, who
was unequal to the occasion.

And then America. Just the raggle-taggle of traffic and
taxis that collects at the west end of the Forties when a liner
comes in, but his, his fatherland. In the year past, the sight
of one of these big grimacing cars shouldering its way through
the Oxford lanes had been to him a breathing flag, a bugle
blown across a field of grain, and here they were, enough of
them to create a traffic jam, honking and glaring at each other

in the tropical-seeming heat, bunched like grapes and as blatantly colored as birds of paradise. They were outrageous, but made sense; they fitted his eyes. Already England seemed a remote, gray apparition. It seemed three years and not three months since he had sat alone in the two-and-six seats of the American-style cinema in Oxford and cried. Joanne had just had the baby. She slept a tuppenny bus ride away, in a hospital bed, to whose foot was attached a basket containing Corinne. All the mothers in the ward seemed to have something wrong with them. They were Irish or American, unwed or unwell. One garrulous crone, tubercular, was frequently milked by a sputtering machine. In the bed beside Joanne, a young colleen wept all day long because her immigrating husband had not yet found work. In visiting hours he nested his snub face on the sheets beside her and they cried together. Joanne had cried when they told her that healthy women were asked to have their babies at home; their home was a dank basement flat in which they leaped from one tight island of heat to another. She had burst into tears, right there at the head of the queue, and the welfare state had clasped her to its drab and ample bosom. They gave her coupons to trade for powdered orange juice. They wrapped the newborn baby in swaddling bands. All he could see of Corinne was her head, a livid red ball, blazing with his blood. It was all very strange. At sunset a parson came into the ward and led an Anglican service that made the mothers cry. Then the husbands came, carrying little bags of fruit and candy bars. Bunched in the waiting room, they could see their wives primping in their cranked-up beds. Then the seven-o'clock bells rang now here, now there, all over the city. When the eight-o'clock bells rang, Joanne gave Robert a passionate kiss, hard with panic yet soft with the wish to sleep. She slept, and a mile away he watched a Doris Day movie about that mythical Midwestern town Hollywood keeps somewhere among its sets. The houses were white, the porches deep, the lawns green, the sidewalks swept, the maples dark and blowzy against the streetlights. Doris Day's upper lip lifted in just that small-town way; her voice cracked. Abruptly, right there in the midst of the rustling Kit Kat bars and stunted shopgirl doxies and young British toughs in their sinister liveries of black, he discovered himself, to his amazement and delight, crying, crying hot honest tears for his lost home.

And then the gritty snarl of customs, and watching the

baggage slide piece by piece down the roller ramp, and trying
to soothe the sweating infant, who had never known such
heat. The badged cherubim who guarded the gate to the
nation allowed him to pass through and give the child to the
grandparents and great-aunts and cousins that waited on the
other side. His mother rose and kissed him on the cheek, and
with an averted glance his father shook his hand, and his
parents-in-law mimicked them, and the other relatives made
appropriate motions of affection, and then they all wandered
about the dismal, resonant waiting room in the desperate little
circles of delay. While he had been abroad, his mother's letters—graceful, witty, informative, cheerful—had been his
main link with home, but now that he saw his parents in the
flesh, it was his father who interested him. His mother had
aged a little; her face was wide, kind, flushed, tense, and
touching—the face of a woman whose country has never quite
settled what to do with its women. And to the extent that she
was clever and civilized, she was European, and a familiar
story.

It was his father who struck him as new, as a potential
revelation. There had been nothing like him in Europe. Old,
incredibly old—he had had all sixteen remaining teeth pulled
while Robert was away, and his face seemed jaundiced with
pain and partially collapsed—he still stood perfectly erect,
like a child that has just learned to stand, his hands held
limply, forward from his body, at the level of his belt. Unwilling, or unable, to look long at his only son or his infant
granddaughter, he explored the waiting room, studying the
water fountain, and a poster for Manischewitz wine, and the
buttons on the coat of a colored porter, as if each might contain the clue to something he had lost. Though for thirty years
a public-school teacher, he still believed in education. Now he
engaged the porter in conversation, gesturing sadly with his
hands, asking questions, questions Robert could not hear but
that he knew from experience could be about anything—the
tonnage of great ships, the popularity of Manischewitz wine,
the mechanics of unloading luggage. The receipt of any information made his father for a brief moment less mournful.
The porter looked up, puzzled and wary at first, and then, the
way it usually went, became flattered and voluble. People in
passing, for all their haste, turned their heads to stare at the
strange duet of the tall, yellow-faced, stubbornly nodding
man in rolled-up shirtsleeves and the dissertating little Negro.
The porter fetched one of his colleagues over to confirm a

point. There was much waving of hands and their voices began to grow loud. Robert's face smarted with the familiar prickles of embarrassment. His father was always so conspicuous. He was so tall that he had been chosen, on the occasion of another return from Europe, to be Uncle Sam and lead their town's Victory Parade in the autumn of 1945.

At last he rejoined the rest of the family and announced, "That was a very interesting man. He said these signs all around saying 'No Tipping' are strictly baloney. He said his union has been fighting for years to get them taken down." He offered this news with a mild air of hope, forming the words hurriedly around his unaccustomed false teeth. Robert made an exasperated noise and turned his back. There. Not in the country one hour and already he had been rude to his father. He returned to the other side of the gate and completed the formalities.

They maneuvered the baggage into the trunk of his father's black '49 Plymouth. The little car looked dusty and vulnerable amid the vibrant taxis. A young blond cop came over to protest its illegal position at the curb and ended, so seductive was the appeal of his father's stoic bewilderment, by helping them lift the huge old-fashioned trunk—Robert's mother's at college —into place among the broken jacks and knots of rope and punctured oil-cans and unraveling wheels of basketball tickets his father carried around. It stuck out over the bumper. They tied the door of the car trunk down with frayed ropes. His father asked the policeman how many taxicabs there were in Manhattan and if it was true, as he had read, that the drivers had been robbed so often they wouldn't go into Harlem at night any more. Their discussion continued throughout the farewells. Robert's aunt, with a kiss that smelled of Kool cigarettes and starched linen, went off to catch the train to Stamford. His cousin, her son, walked away under the pillars of the West Side Highway; he lived on West Twelfth Street and worked as an animator for television commercials. His wife's parents herded their little flock of kin toward the parking lot, redeemed their scarlet Volvo, and began the long haul to Boston. Mother got into the front seat of the Plymouth. Robert and Joanne and Corinne arranged themselves in the back. Minutes passed; then his father and the policeman parted, and his father got in behind the wheel. "That was very interesting," he said. "He said ninety-nine out of a hundred Puerto Ricans are honest." With a doleful thump of the clutch, they headed for Pennsylvania.

Robert had a job teaching mathematics to ex-debutantes at a genteel college on the Hudson. It would begin in September. This was July. For the interval, they were to sponge off their parents. His got them first. He had looked forward to this month; it would be the longest he would have been in Pennsylvania with his wife, and he had a memory of something he had wanted to describe, to explain, to her about his home. But exactly what that was, he had forgotten. His parents lived in a small town fifty miles west of Philadelphia, in a thickly German county. His mother had been born in the county, on a farm, and felt involved with the land but estranged from its people. His father had come from the center of Baltimore, and groped after people, but saw no comfort in land. Whereas Robert, who had been born and raised in the small town, where people and land made a patchwork, thought he loved both; yet ever since he could remember, he had been planning to escape. The air, the people, had seemed too thick, too apt to choke him. He had made that escape. It had seemed necessary. But it had left him feeling hollow, fragile, transparent— a vial waiting to be filled with tears by the next Doris Day movie. Coming home filled him with strength, a thicker liquid. But each time less full; he sensed this. Both he and the land were altering. The container was narrowing; the thing contained was growing impure. In the year past, his mother's letters had often seemed enigmatic and full of pale, foreign matter. So it was with a sense of guilty urgency that he silently urged the car forward, as if the heart of America might give out before he reached it.

His father said, "That cop told me he had studied to be a television repairman but couldn't get any business so he became a cop. He said the field's gotten crowded as hell in the last five years."

"Daddy, hush," Mother said. "The baby wants to go to sleep."

Corinne had been terrorized by the tooting of the tugboats; being passed from arms to arms had sustained her upset. Now she lay on the floor of the car in a cream-colored Carry-Cot they had bought in England. Just looking at its nickel studs and braces made Robert remember the carriage shop on the Cowley Road, with its bright black rows of stately prams built as if for a lifetime; and indeed the English did wheel their children around until they were immense. Ah, the dear, rosy English; he began, with a soft reversal of blood, to feel homesick for them. Could he never rest?

They undressed Corinne of her woolen clothes and she lay in a diaper, pink with heat, kicking her legs and whimpering. Then the whorls of her face slumped sideways, her star-shaped hands stopped fidgeting, and she fell asleep on the jiggling bosom of the highway. "Honestly, Joanne," Robert's mother said, "I've never seen such a perfect baby. And I'm not just being a mother-in-law when I say that." Her protest was abrasive on several sides; Robert resisted the implication that the baby had been solely Joanne's doing.

"I like her bellybutton," he asserted.

"It's a masterpiece," his mother said, and he felt, in a queer way, confirmed. But even then: the baby's beauty, like all beauty, was self-enclosed, and led nowhere. Their talk stayed shy and tentative. There was gossip between Robert and his parents that his wife could not share; and a growing body of allusions between himself and Joanne to which his parents were aliens. The widening range and importance of these allusions, which could not by any effort of politeness be completely suppressed, seemed to dwindle and mock his relation with his parents. He had always, even at college age, smoked *suh rosa*, out of the house, where the sight would not offend his mother. It had been like making love: forgivable but unsightly. But now, as Joanne burned Player after Player in her nervousness at his father's eccentric and preoccupied driving, he could not, as her husband and as a man, abstain; and anyway, of the two old sins it had been the lesser, and the fruit of the worse had just been praised. At the scratch of his match, his mother turned her head and looked at him levelly. To her credit, there was not a tremor of reproach. Yet after that level look he was painfully conscious of the smoke that drifted forward and encircled her head, and of the patient way she kept brushing it from her face with her hand. Her hand was freckled on the back and her wedding ring cut deeply into the flesh of the third finger, giving her quietest gesture a passive, wounded eloquence.

It seemed a point scored for her side when Joanne, panicked that her father-in-law would bungle the turnoff for the Pulaski Skyway, shattered the tip of her cigarette against the back of the seat and a live ash fell on the baby's belly. It went unnoticed for a second, until Corinne screamed; then they all saw it, a little flea of fire glowing beside the perfect navel. Joanne jumped, and squealed with guilt, and flapped her hands and stamped her feet and hugged the baby against her, but the evidence could not be destroyed; a brown dot of

char on the globe of immaculate skin. Corinne continued her
screams, splicing them with shrill hard gasps of intake,
while everyone rummaged through purses and pockets for
Vaseline, butter, toothpaste—anything for an unguent. Mother
had a tiny bottle of toilet water given her in a department
store; Joanne dabbed some of this on, and in time Corinne,
shaken by more and more widely spaced spasms of sobbing,
mercifully dragged her injury with her into the burrow of
sleep.

The incident was so like the incident of the penny that
Robert had to tell them about it. On the boat he had gone
down to their cabin, where Corinne was sleeping, to get his
wallet from his other coat. The coat was hanging on a hook
over her crib. The tourist cabins on these big liners, he
explained, are terribly cramped—everything on top of everything else.

His father nodded, swallowing a fact. "They don't give you
much space, huh?"

"They *can't*," Robert told him. "Anyway, in my hurry or
something, when I took out the wallet I flipped an English
penny out and it flew and hit Corinne right in the center of
her forehead."

"Why, Robert!" Mother said.

"Oh, it was awful. She cried for an hour. Much longer
than just now, with the spark."

"She must be getting used to our dropping things on her,"
Joanne said.

With a possibly pointed tact, his mother declined to agree
with this suggestion, and expressed politely exaggerated interest in the English penny they showed her. Why it *is* heavy!
And is this the *smallest* denomination? They eagerly showed
her other British coins. But there were elements in the story
that had been suppressed: they had needed his wallet because
they had used up all their change in an uproarious orgy of
blackjack and beer. And from Joanne, even, Robert had this
secret: the reason for his haste in retrieving the wallet was
his hurry to get back to the invigorating company of the flashy
and rather dumb but quite good-looking girl from Virginia
who had boarded the boat at Cobh. In the dim cabin, lit by a
blue bulb and heated with his lust, the weird flight of the
penny had seemed a judgment.

So the accident, and the anecdote, reinforced the constraint.
The dear stucco hot-dog stands, the beloved white frame
houses, the fervently stocked and intimately cool drugstores

unfurled behind car windows smeared with sullen implications of guilt, disappointment, apology, and lost time. Robert looked to his parents to break the spell. Married, employed, in a narrow way learned, himself a father, he was still childish enough to expect his parents to pierce the many little mysteries that had been deposited between them; to make a miracle. He blamed them for failing to do it. In their infinite power they had only to stretch out a hand. Spitefully he began to look forward to the month in Boston they would spend with *her* parents.

They came west across New Jersey, crossed the Delaware where Washington had once crossed it, and on a southwesterly curve penetrated into Pennsylvania. The towns along the route changed from the flat, wooden New Jersey sort, with their fragile prairie flavor of languor and dust, into a stiffer, more Teutonic type, braced against hills with stone and brick, laid out stubbornly on the plan of a grid, though this dogmatism compelled extensive sustaining walls that rose and fell with the land, damming brief domed lawns crowned with narrow brick houses whose basement windows were higher than the top of their car. The brutal sun passed noon; the trunk lid rattled and bobbed as the ropes loosened. They came to the border of the ten or twenty square miles that Robert knew well. In this town he had gone each fall to a football game, and in this one he had attended a fair where the girls in the tents danced wearing nothing but high-heeled lavender shoes.

A web began to clog Robert's throat. He sneezed. "Poor Robbie," his mother said. "I bet he hasn't had hay fever since the last time he was home."

"I didn't know he got hay fever," Joanne said.

"Oh, terribly," his mother said. "When he was a little boy, it used to break my heart. With his sinuses, he really shouldn't smoke."

They all swayed; a car at the curb had unexpectedly nosed into their path, and his father, without touching the brake, swung around it. It was a long green car, glitteringly new, and the face at the driver's window, suspended for a moment like a rubber ball on the wave of their swerve, was startled and pink. Robert noticed this dully. His eyes were watering. They drove on, and a half-mile passed before the swelling honking dawned on him as aimed at them. The green car was speeding to catch them; it rode a few yards behind their bumper while the driver leaned on the horn. Robert turned and through the rear window read, between the triple headlights hooded under twirled eyebrows of metal, the tall letters OLDSMOBILE embodied in the grille. The car surged into the next lane and slowed to their speed; it was extravagantly streamlined and its sweepback windshield gave it the look of losing its hat. The little red driver screamed over through the near window. The man's middle-aged wife, as if she were often a partner in this performance, expertly pulled back her head to let his words fly past, but they were indistinguishable in the rush of wind and whirling rubber.

Daddy turned to Mother; he was squinting in pain. "What's he saying, Julia? I can't hear what he's saying." He still looked to his wife now and then as his interpreter in this region, though he had lived here thirty years.

"He's saying he's an angry man," Mother said.

Robert, his brain fogged by the gathering gasps of a sneeze, stamped on the floor, to make their car travel faster and outrace their assailant. But his father slowed and braked to a stop.

The Olds was taken by surprise, and travelled a good distance beyond them before it, too, pulled over to the side of the road. They were outside the town; beautiful trim farmland, hazy with pollen, undulated in the heat on either side of the highway. The car up ahead spat out its driver. At a fat little trot a short squat man jogged back along the gravel shoulder toward them. He wore a flowered Hawaiian shirt and words were spilling from his mouth. The motor of the old Plymouth, too hot to idle after four hours of steady running, throbbed and stalled. The man's head arrived at the side window; he had a square skull, with ridges of cartilage above the tiny white ears, and his skin, flushed and puckered as it was by raving, gave an impression of lambent delicacy, like the skin on a sausage. Even before the man regained his breath to speak, Robert recognized him as a prime specimen of the breed that the outside world with ignorant fondness calls the Pennsylvania Dutch. And then, in the first shrill cascade of outrage, the juicy *ch*'s and misplaced *w*'s of the accent seemed visually distinct, like letters stamped on shattered crates sliding down a waterfall. As the wild voice lowered and slowed, whole strings of obscenities were explicit. Consecutive sentences could be understood. "You hat no right to cut me off like that. Youff no right to go through town like that." Robert's father made no answer; this refusal whipped the little red man into a new spin of fury: his skin shining as if to burst, he thrust his face into their window; he shut his eyes and his eyelids swelled; the wings of his nostrils whitened with pressure. His voice broke, as if frightened of itself, and he turned his back and walked a step away. His movements in the brilliant air seemed managed against a huge and impelling rigidity.

Robert's father mildly called after him, "I'm trying to understand you, mister, but I can't catch your meaning. I can't get your point."

This gave the top another turn, more furious still, but of shorter duration. Mother brushed some smoke from her face, relieving a long paralysis. The baby whimpered, and Joanne moved to the edge of the seat, trying to confront the source of the disturbance. Perhaps these motions from the women stirred feelings of guilt in the Dutchman; he released, like an ancillary legal argument, another spasm of lavatory-wall words, and his bright white hands did a galvanized dance among the flowers of his shirt, and he actually, like a dervish, whirled completely around. Mournfully Robert's father gazed into the vortex, the skin of his face going increasingly yellow, as if with repeated extractions. In profile his lips clamped stubbornly over his clumsy teeth, and his eye was a perfect diamond of undeviating interest. This attentiveness dragged at the Dutchman's indignant momentum. The aggrieved and obscene voice, which in the strange acoustics of the noon seemed to be echoing off the baking blue plate above them all, halted with a scratch of friction.

As if the spark had just struck her belly, Corinne began to scream. Joanne crouched down and shouted toward the front window, "You've woken up the baby!"

Robert's legs ached, and, partly to stretch them, partly to show indignation, he opened his door and got out. He felt his slender height, encased in his black English suit, unfold like an elegant and surprising weapon. The enemy's beaded forehead puckered doubtfully. "Whawereya trine to pull aat in front of us for?" Robert asked him in the slouching accents of home. His voice, stoppered by hay fever and dwindled by the blatant sunlight, seemed less his own than that of an old acquaintance.

His father opened his door and got out also. At the revelation of this even greater, more massive height, the Dutchman spat on the asphalt, taking care not to hit any shoes. Still working against that invisible resistance in the air, he jerkily pivoted and began to strut toward his car.

"No, wait a minute, mister," Robert's father called, and began to stride after him. The pink face, abruptly drained of fury, flashed above the soaked shoulder of the Hawaiian shirt. The Dutchman went into his trot. Robert's father, in his anxiety at seeing a conversation broken off, gave chase; his lengthening stride lifted his body off the ground with an awesome, floating slow motion. Under the shimmer of the road his shadow seemed to be falling away from his feet. His voice drifted faintly down the glaring highway. "Wait a minute, mister. I want to ask you something." As the perspective closed the distance between them, the Dutchman's legs twittered like a pinioned insect's, but this was an illusion; he was not caught. He arrived at the door of his Oldsmobile; judged he had time to utter one more curse, uttered it, and dodged into the glistening green shell. Robert's father arrived at the bumper as the car pulled out. The tense wrinkles on the back of his shirt implied an urge to hurl himself upon the fleeing metal. Then the wrinkles relaxed as he straightened his shoulders.

Erect with frustration, arms swinging, he marched down the side of the road just as fifteen years before, in spats and a top hat made of cardboard, he had marched at the head of that parade.

Inside the car, Joanne was jiggling the baby and giggling. She had never seen her father-in-law succeed before. "That was wonderful," she said.

With an effort of contraction he shrank into his place behind the steering wheel. He started the car and turned his big head sadly to tell her, "No. That man had something to say to me and I wanted to hear what it was. If I did something wrong, I want to know about it. But the bastard wouldn't talk sense. Like everybody else in this country; I can't understand them. They're Julia's people."

"I think he thought we were gypsies," Mother said. "On account of the old trunk in the back. Also the lid was up and he couldn't see our Pennsylvania license plate. They're very anxious, you know, to keep the 'impure races' out of this section. And then Daddy's skin confused him. Once the poor fellow heard us talk, he was satisfied."

"He seemed awfully mad about nothing," Joanne said.

Mother's voice quickened, became fluid. "Well that's how they *are,* Joanne. The people in this part of the country are just mad all the time. God gave them these beautiful valleys and they're hopping mad. I don't know why. I think there's too much starch in their diet." Her dietary theories were close to her heart; her touching on them conferred on Joanne a daughter's status.

Robert called forward, "Daddy, I don't think he really had any information." He spoke partly to hear his old voice again, partly to compete for attention with his newly created sibling, and partly in a vain hope of gathering to himself some of the glory his father now and then won in the course of his baffled quest; but primarily he spoke to show his wife how accustomed he was to such scenes, how often such triumphant catastrophes had entered his life at home, so that he could be quite blasé about them. This was not true: he was intensely excited, and grew even more so as in folds of familiarity the land tightened around him.

Archangel

Onyx and split cedar and bronze vessels lowered into still water: these things I offer. Porphyry, teakwood, jasmine, and myrrh: these gifts I bring. The sheen of my sandals is dulled by the dust of cloves. My wings are waxed with nectar. My eyes are diamonds in whose facets red gold is mirrored. My face is a mask of ivory: Love me. Listen to my promises:

Cold water will drip from the intricately chased designs of the bronze vessels. Thick-lipped urns will sweat in the fragrant cellars. The orchards never weary of bearing on my islands. The very leaves give nourishment. The banked branches never crowd the paths. The grape vines will grow unattended. The very seeds of the berries are sweet nuts. Why do you smile? Have you never been hungry?

The workmanship of the bowers will be immaculate. Where the elements are joined, the sword of the thinnest whisper will find its point excluded. Where the beams have been tapered, each swipe of the plane is continuous. Where the wood needed locking, pegs of a counter grain have been driven. The ceilings are high, for coolness, and the spaced shingles seal at the first breath of mist. Though the windows are open, the eaves of the roof are so wide that nothing of the rain comes into the rooms but its scent. Mats of perfect cleanness cover the floor. The fire is cupped in black rock and sustained on a smooth breast of ash. Have you never lacked shelter?

Where, then, has your life been touched? My pleasures are as specific as they are everlasting. The sliced edges of a fresh ream of laid paper, cream, stiff, rag-rich. The freckles of the closed eyelids of a woman attentive in the first white blush of morning. The ball diminishing well down the broad green throat of the first at Cape Ann. The good catch, a candy sun slatting the bleachers. The fair at the vanished poorhouse. The white arms of girls dancing, taffeta, white arms violet in the hollows music its ecstasies praise the white wrists of praise the white arms and the white paper trimmed the Euclidean proof of Pythagoras' theorem its tightening beauty the iridescence of an old copper found in the salt sand. The microscopic glitter in the ink of the letters of words that are your own. Certain moments, remembered or imagined, of childhood. Three-handed pinochle by the brown glow of the stained-glass lampshade, your parents out of their godliness silently wishing you to win. The Brancusi room, silent. *Pines and Rocks,* by Cézanne; and The Lace-Maker in the Louvre hardly bigger than your spread hand.

Such glimmers I shall widen to rivers; nothing will be lost, not the least grain of remembered dust, and the multiplication shall be a thousand thousand fold; love me. Embrace me; come, touch my side, where honey flows. Do not be afraid. Why should my promises be vain? Jade and cinnamon: do you deny that such things exist? Why do you turn away? Is not my song a stream of balm? My arms are heaped with apples and ancient books; there is no harm in me; no. Stay. Praise me. Your praise of me is praise of yourself; wait. Listen. I will begin again.

You'll Never Know, Dear,
How Much I Love You

CARNIVAL! In the vacant lot beyond the old ice plant! Trucks have been unloading all afternoon; the Whirlo-Gig has been unfolded like a giant umbrella, they assembled the baby Ferris wheel with an Erector Set. Twice the trucks got stuck in the mud. Straw has been strewn everywhere. They put up a stage and strung lights. Now, now, gather your pennies; supper is over and an hour of light is left in the long summer day. See, Sammy Hunnenhauser is running; Gloria Gring and her gang have been there all afternoon, they never go home, oh hurry, let me go; how awful it is to have parents that are poor, and slow, and sad!

Fifty cents. The most Ben could beg. A nickel for every year of his life. It feels like plenty. Over the roof of crazy Mrs. Moffert's house, the Ferris wheel tints the air with pink, and the rim of this pink mixes in excitement with the great notched rim of the coin sweating in his hand. This house, then this house, and past the ice plant, and he will be there. Already the rest of the world is there, he is the last, hurrying, hurrying, the balloon is about to take off, the Ferris wheel is lifting; only he will be left behind, on empty darkening streets.

Then there, what to buy? There are not so many people here. Grownups carrying babies mosey glassily on the straw walks. All the booth people, not really gypsies, stare at him, and beckon weakly. It hurts him to ignore the man with the three old softballs, and the old cripple at the merry-go-round, and the fat lady with her plaster Marys, and the skeleton suspended behind a fountain of popcorn. He feels his walking past them as pain. He wishes there were more people here; he feels a fool. All of this machinery assembled to extract from him his pathetic fifty cents. He watches at a distance a thickset man in earnestly rolled-up shirtsleeves twirl a great tinselled wheel with a rubber tongue that patters slower and slower on a circle of nails until it stops between two, and the number there wins. Only a sailor and two boys in yellow silk high-school athletic jackets play. None win. The thick tattooed arm below the rolled-up shirtsleeve carefully sweeps their nickels from a long board divided and numbered as if for hopscotch. The high-school boys, with sideburns and spotty whiskers on their bright pink jaws, put down nickels again leadenly, and this time the man spinning the wheel shouts when it stops, seems more joyful than they, and reaches into his deep apron pocket and pours before them, without counting, a perfect little slipping stack of nickels. Their gums showing as if at a dirty joke, the two boys turn— the shimmer on their backs darts and shifts in cool z's—and walk away, while the man is shouting, "Hey, uh winneh. Hey, uh winneth, evvybody wins." His table is bare, and as his mouth continues to form the loud words his eyes lock Ben into a stare of heartbreaking brown blankness that seems to elucidate with paralyzing clarity Ben's state: his dungarees, his fifty cents, his ten years, his position in space, and above the particulars the immense tinted pity, the waste, of being at one little place instead of everywhere, at any time. Then the man looks away, and twirls the wheel for his own amusement.

The fifty-cent piece feels huge to Ben's fingers, a wide oppressive rigidity that must be broken, shattered into twinkling fragments, to merge in the tinsel and splinters of strewn straw. He buys, at the first stand he strikes, a cone of cotton candy, and receives, with the furry pink pasty uncoiling thing, a quarter, a dime, and a nickel: three coins, tripling his wealth.

Now people multiply, crowd in from the houses of the town, that stand beyond the lot on all sides in black forbidding silhouettes like the teeth of a saw. The lights go on; the faces of the houses flee. There is nothing in the lot but light, and at its core, on the stage, three girls wearing white cowboy hats and white spangled skirts and white boots appear, and a man also in white and bearing a white guitar strung with gold. The legs around Ben crush him toward the stage; the smell of mud mingles with the bright sight there. One of the girls coughs into the microphone and twists its neck, so a sharp whine pierces from the loudspeakers and cuts a great crescent through the crowd, leaving silence as harvest. The girls sing, toetapping gingerly: "The other *night,* dear, as I lay *sleep*ing, I dreamt I *held* you in my *arms.*" The spangles on their swishing skirts spring prickles like tears in Ben's eyes. The three voices sob, catch, twang, distend his heart like a rubber band at the highest pitch of their plaint. "—I was mis*tak*en, and I *hung* my *head,* a-and *cried.*" And then the unbearable rising sugar of the chorus that makes his scalp so tight he fears his head will burst from sweet fullness.

The girls go on to sing other songs, less good, and then they give way to a thin old man in suspenders and huge pants he keeps snapping and looking down and whooping into. He tells horrible jokes that make the nice fat ladies standing around Ben—nice fat factory and dustmop women that made him feel protected—shake with laughter. He fears their quaking, feels threatened from beneath, as if there is a treacherous stratum under this mud and straw. He wanders away, to let the words of "You Are My Sunshine" revolve in his head. "Please don't *take* my *sun*shine a*way.*" Only the money in his pocket weighs him; get rid of it, and he will sail away like a dandelion seed.

He goes to the booth where the wheel is turning, and puts his nickel on the board in a square marked 7, and loses it.

He puts the dime there and it too is taken away.

Squeezed, almost hidden, between the crusty trousered haunches of two adults, he puts down his quarter, as they do, on the inner edge, to be changed. The tattooed man comes along picking up the quarters and pouring, with his wonderfully automatic fingers, the little slipping stacks of five nickels; Ben holds his breath, and to his horror feels his low face catch in the corner of the man's absent-minded eyes. The thick solemn body snags in its smooth progress, and Ben's five nickels are raggedly spaced. Between the second and third there is a gap. A blush cakes Ben's cheeks; his gray-knuckled fingers, as they push out a nickel, are trembling sideways at each other. But the man goes back, and spins the wheel, and Ben loses three nickels one after another. The twittering wheel is a moon-faced god; but Ben feels humanity clouding the space between them, that should be unobstructed. When the tattooed arm—a blue fish, an anchor, the queer word PEACE—comes to sweep in his nickels, he feels stippled skin breathing thought, and lowers his head against the expected fall of words. Nothing is said, the man moves on, returns to the wheel; but Ben feels puzzled pressure radiating from him, and the pointed eyes of a man in a suit with chalk stripes who has come to stand at the far side of the stand intersect this expanding circle, and Ben, hurrying to pour his money down a narrowing crack, puts down his last two nickels, still on 7.

The rubber tongue leaps into pattering and as the wheel whirls the tattooed man leans backward to hear the one in chalk stripes talk; his tongue patters silently but a tiny motion of his polished hand, simultaneous with a sideways stab of his eyes, is toward Ben.

The rubber tongue slows, flops, stops at 7—no, 8. He lost, and can leave. The floor of his stomach lifts queerly. "Hey kid." The man with stencilled arms comes over. Ben feels that no matter how fast he would run, those arms would stretch and snare him.

"Huh?"

"How old are you, kid?"

"Ten."

"Whatsamatta with ya, ya daddy rich?"

A titter moves stiffly through the immense adult heads all around. Ben understands the familiar role, that he has undergone a hundred times with teachers and older boys, of being a comic prop. He understands everything, and wants to explain that he knows his eyes are moist and his cheeks red but that it's because of joy, freedom, not because of losing. But this would be too many words; even the one-word answer "No" sticks to the roof of his mouth and comes loose with a faint tearing noise.

"Here." With his exciting expert touch, the man flicks Ben's two coins back across the painted number. Then he digs into his pocket. He comes up with the usual little stack of five, drops four, but holds the fifth delicately between the tips of two fingers and a thumb, hesitates so that Ben can reread PEACE in blue above his wrist, and then flips the fifth nickel up into his palm and thence down with a plunge into his dirty sagging apron pouch.

"Now move away from the board, kid, move away. Don't come back."

Ben fumbles the coins into his hands and pushes away, his eyes screwed to the sharp edge of painted wood, and shoulders blindly backward through the legs. Yet all the time, in the midst of the heat and water welling up from springs all over his body, he is figuring, and calculates he's been gypped. Forty: he had the quarter and dime and nickel and they gave him back only six nickels: thirty. The injustice, they pretend he's too little to lose and then keep a dime; the waste. The lost dime seems a tiny hole through which everything in existence is draining. As he moves away, his wet knees jarring, trying to hide forever from every sailor and fat woman and high-schooler who witnessed his disgrace, the six nickels make a knobbed weight bumping his thigh through his pocket. The spangles, the splinters of straw and strings of light, the sawtooth peaks of houses showing behind the scattered white heads scented sweetly with mud, are hung like the needles of a Christmas tree with the transparent, tinted globes confusing his eyelashes.

Thus the world, like a bitter coquette, spurns our attempts to give ourselves to her wholly.

The Astronomer

I FEARED HIS VISIT. I was twenty-four, and the religious revival within myself was at its height. Earlier that summer, I had discovered Kierkegaard, and each week I brought back to the apartment one more of the Princeton University Press's elegant and expensive editions of his works. They were beautiful books, sometimes very thick, sometimes very thin, always typographically exhilarating, with their welter of title pages, subheads, epigraphs, emphatic italics, italicized catchwords taken from German philosophy and too subtle for translation, translator's prefaces and footnotes, and Kierkegaard's own endless footnotes, blanketing pages at a time as, crippled, agonized by distinctions, he scribbled on and on, heaping irony on irony, curse on curse, gnashing, sneering, praising Jehovah in the privacy of his empty home in Copenhagen. The demons with which he wrestled—Hegel and his avatars —were unknown to me, so Kierkegaard at his desk seemed to me to be writhing in the clutch of phantoms, slapping at silent mosquitoes, twisting furiously to confront presences that were not there. It was a spectacle unlike any I had ever seen in print before, and it brought me much comfort during those August and September evenings, while the traffic on the West Side Highway swished tirelessly and my wife tinkled the supper dishes in our tiny kitchenette.

We lived at the time on the sixth floor of a building on Riverside Drive, and overlooked the Hudson. The river would become black before the sky, and the little Jersey towns on the far bank would be pinched between two massive tongs of darkness until only a row of sparks remained. These embers were reflected in the black water, and when a boat went dragging its wake up the river the reflections would tremble, double, fragment, and not until long after the shadow of the boat passed reconstruct themselves.

125

The astronomer was a remnant of our college days. Two years had passed since we had seen him. When Harriet and I were both undergraduates, another couple, a married couple, had introduced him to us. The wife of this couple had gone to school with Harriet, and the husband was a teaching associate of the astronomer; so Bela and I were the opposite ends of a chain. He was a Hungarian. His parents had fled the terror of Kun's regime; they were well-to-do. From Vienna they had come to London; from there Bela had gone to Oxford, and from there come to this country, years ago. He was forty, a short, thickset man with a wealth of stiff black hair, combed straight back without a parting, like a Slav bicyclist. Only a few individuals hairs had turned white. He gave an impression of abnormal density; his anatomical parts seemed set one on top of the other without any loose space between for leeway or accommodation of his innards. A motion in his foot instantly jerked his head. The Magyar cheekbones gave his face a blunt, aggressive breadth; he wore steel-rimmed glasses that seemed several sizes too small. He was now teaching at Columbia. Brilliant, he rarely deigned to publish papers, so that his brilliance was carried around with him as undiminished potency. He liked my wife. Like Kierkegaard, he was a bachelor, and in the old days his flirtatious compliments, rolled out with a rich, slow British accent and a broad-mouthed, thoughtful smile across a cafeteria table or after dinner in our friends' living room, made me feel foolish and incapable; she was not my wife then. "Ah, Harri-et, Harri-et," he would call, giving the last syllable of her name a full, French, roguish weight, "come and sit by me on this Hide-a-bed." And then he would pat the cushion beside him, which his own weight had caused to lift invitingly. Somewhat more than a joke, it was nevertheless not rude to me; I did not have enough presence in his eyes to receive rudeness.

He had an air of seeing beyond me, of seeing into the interstellar structure of things, of having transcended, except perhaps in the niggling matter of lust, the clouds of human subjectivity—vaporous hopes supported by immaterial rationalizations. It was his vigorous, clear vision that I feared.

When he came into our apartment, directing warmth into all its corners with brisk handshakes and abrupt pivotings of his whole frame, he spotted the paperback *Meno* that I had been reading, back and forth on the subway, two pages per stop. It is the dialogue in which Socrates, to demonstrate the existence of indwelling knowledge, elicits some geometrical truths from a small boy. "My Lord, Walter," Bela said, "why are you reading this? Is this the one where he proves two and two equals four?" And thus quickly, at a mere wink from this atheist, Platonism and all its attendant cathedrals came tumbling down.

We ate dinner by the window, from which the Hudson appeared a massive rent opened in a tenuous web of light. Though we talked trivially, about friends and events, I felt the structure I had painstakingly built up within myself wasting away; my faith (existentialism padded out with Chesterton), my prayers, my churchgoing (to a Methodist edifice where the spiritual void of the inner city reigned above the fragile hats of a dozen old ladies and the minister shook my hand at the door with a look of surprise on his face), all dwindled to the thinnest filaments of illusion, and in one flash, I knew, they would burn to nothing. I felt behind his eyes immensities of space and gas, seemed to see with him through my own evanescent body into gigantic systems of dead but furious matter, suns like match heads, planets like cinders, galaxies that were whirls of ash, and beyond them, more galaxies, and more, fleeing with sickening speed beyond the rim that our most powerful telescopes could reach. I had once heard him explain, in a cafeteria, how the white dwarf star called the companion of Sirius is so dense that light radiating from it is tugged back by gravitation toward the red end of the spectrum.

My wife took our dessert dishes away; before she brought coffee, I emptied the last of the red wine into our glasses. Bela lit a cigar and, managing its fresh length and the wineglass with his electric certainty of touch, talked. Knowing that, since the principal business of my employment was to invent the plots of television commercials, I was to some extent a humorist, he told me of a parody he had seen of the B.B.C. Third Programme. It involved Bertrand Russell reading the first five hundred decimal places of π, followed by twenty minutes of silent meditation led by Mr. T. S. Eliot, and then Bertrand Russell reading the *next* five hundred places of π.

If my laughter burst out excessively, it was because his acknowledgment, though minimal and oblique, that Bertrand Russell might by some conception be laughable and that meditation and the author of "Little Gidding" did at least *exist* momentarily relieved me of the strain of maintaining against the pressure of his latent opinions my own superstitious, fainthearted identity. This small remission of his field of force admitted worlds of white light, and my wife, returning to the room holding with bare arms at the level of our eyes a tray on which an old tin pot and three china demitasse cups stated their rectangular silhouettes, seemed a creature of intense beauty.

"Ah, Harri-et, Harri-et," Bela said, lowering his cigar, "married life has not dimmed thy lustre."

My wife blushed, rather too readily—her skin had always been discomfitingly quick to answer his praise—and set the tray on the table and took her chair and served us. Mixing wine and coffee in our mouths, we listened to Bela tell of when he first came to this country. He was an instructor in general science at a university in Michigan. The thermometer stayed at zero for months, the students carved elaborate snow sculptures on the campus, everyone wore ear muffs and un-buckled galoshes. At first, he couldn't believe in the ear muffs; they looked like something you would find among the most secluded peasantry of Central Europe. It had taken him months to muster the courage to go into a shop and ask for such childish things. But at last he had, and had been very happy in them. They were very sensible. He continued to wear them, though in the East they did not seem to be the fashion.

"I know," Harriet said. "In the winter here, you see all these poor Madison Avenue men—"

"Such as Walter," Bela smoothly interceded, shaping his cigar ash on the edge of his saucer.

"Well, yes, except it doesn't look so bad with him because he never cuts his hair. But all these other men with their tight little hats on the top of their haircuts right in the dead of this damp, windy winter—their ears are bright red in the subway."

"And the girls," Bela said, "the girls in the Midwest wear *immense puffs,* as big around as—" He cupped his hands, fingers spread, over his ears and, hunching his head down on his thick brief neck, darted glances at us in a startled way. He had retained, between two fingers, the cigar, so his head seemed to have sprouted, rather low, one smoking horn. His hands darted away, his chest expanded and became rigid as he tried to embrace, for us, the sense of these remote pompoms. "White, woolly," he said sharply, giving each adjective a lecturer's force; then the words glided as he suddenly exhaled. "They're like the snowballs that girls in your ice shows wear on their breasts." He pronounced the two *s*'s in "breasts" so distinctly it seemed the radiator had hissed.

It surprised us that he had ever seen an ice show. We had not thought of him as a sightseer. But it turned out that in those first years he had inspected the country thoroughly. He had bought an old Dodge one summer and driven all around the West by himself. With incongruous piety, he had visited the Grand Canyon, Yosemite, a Sioux reservation. He described a long stretch of highway in New Mexico. "There are these black hills. Utterly without vegetation. Great, heavy, almost purplish folds, unimaginably ugly, mile after mile after mile. Not a gas station, not a sign of green. Nothing." And his face, turning rapidly from one to the other of us, underwent an expression I had never before seen him wear. His black eyebrows shot up in two arches stretching his eyelids smooth, and his upper lip tightened over his lower, which was retracted in a way that indicated it was being delicately pinched between his teeth. This expression, bestowed in silence and swiftly erased, confessed what he could not pronounce: He had been frightened.

On the table, below our faces, the cups and glasses broken into shards by shadows, the brown dregs of coffee and wine, the ashtrays and the ashes were hastily swept together into a little heap of warm dark tones distinct from the universal debris.

That is all I remember. The mingle on the table was only part of the greater confusion as in the heat of rapport our unrelated spirits and pasts scrambled together, bringing everything in the room with them, including the rubble of footnotes bound into Kierkegaard. In memory, perhaps because we lived on the sixth floor, this scene—this invisible scene—seems to take place at a great height, as if we were the residents of a star suspended against the darkness of the city and the river. What is the past, after all, but a vast sheet of darkness in which a few moments pricked apparently at random, shine?

A & P

IN WALKS these three girls in nothing but bathing suits. I'm
in the third checkout slot, with my back to the door, so I
don't see them until they're over by the bread. The one that
caught my eye first was the one in the plaid green two-piece.
She was a chunky kid, with a good tan and a sweet broad
soft-looking can with those two crescents of white just under
it, where the sun never seems to hit, at the top of the backs
of her legs. I stood there with my hand on a box of HiHo
crackers trying to remember if I rang it up or not. I ring it up
again and the customer starts giving me hell. She's one of
these cash-register-watchers, a witch about fifty with rouge on
her cheekbones and no eyebrows, and I know it made her day
to trip me up. She'd been watching cash registers for fifty
years and probably never seen a mistake before.

By the time I got her feathers smoothed and her goodies
into a bag—she gives me a little snort in passing, if she'd been
born at the right time they would have burned her over in
Salem—by the time I get her on her way the girls had circled
around the bread and were coming back, without a pushcart,
back my way along the counters, in the aisle between the
checkouts and the Special bins. They didn't even have shoes
on. There was this chunky one, with the two-piece—it was
bright green and the seams on the bra were still sharp and
her belly was still pretty pale so I guessed she just got it (the
suit)—there was this one, with one of those chubby berry-
faces, the lips all bunched together under her nose, this one,
and a tall one, with black hair that hadn't quite frizzed right,
and one of these sunburns right across under the eyes, and
a chin that was too long—you know, the kind of girl other
girls think is very "striking" and "attractive" but never quite
makes it, as they very well know, which is why they like her
so much—and then the third one, that wasn't quite so tall.

130

She was the queen. She kind of led them, the other two peeking around and making their shoulders round. She didn't look
around, not this queen, she just walked straight on slowly, on
these long white prima-donna legs. She came down a little
hard on her heels, as if she didn't walk in her bare feet that
much, putting down her heels and then letting the weight move
along to her toes as if she was testing the floor with every
step, putting a little deliberate extra action into it. You never
know for sure how girls' minds work (do you really think
it's a mind in there or just a little buzz like a bee in a glass
jar?) but you got the idea she had talked the other two into
coming in here with her, and now she was showing them how
to do it, walk slow and hold yourself straight.

She had on a kind of dirty-pink—beige maybe, I don't
know—bathing suit with a little nubble all over it, and what
got me, the straps were down. They were off her shoulders
looped loose around the cool tops of her arms, and I guess as a
result the suit had slipped a little on her, so all around the
top of the cloth there was this shining rim. If it hadn't been
there you wouldn't have known there could have been anything whiter than those shoulders. With the straps pushed off,
there was nothing between the top of the suit and the top
of her head except just *her*, this clean bare plane of the top
of her chest down from the shoulder bones like a dented
sheet of metal tilted in the light. I mean, it was more than
pretty.

She had sort of oaky hair that the sun and salt had bleached,
done up in a bun that was unravelling, and a kind of prim
face. Walking into the A & P with your straps down, I suppose it's the only kind of face you *can* have. She held her
head so high her neck, coming up out of those white shoulders, looked kind of stretched, but I didn't mind. The longer
her neck was, the more of her there was.

She must have felt in the corner of her eye me and over
my shoulder Stokesie in the second slot watching, but she
didn't tip. Not this queen. She kept her eyes moving across
the racks, and stopped, and turned so slow it made my stomach
rub the inside of my apron, and buzzed to the other two, who
kind of huddled against her for relief, and then they all three
of them went up the cat-and-dog-food-breakfast-cereal-
macaroni-rice-raisins-seasonings-spreads-spaghetti-soft-drinks-
crackers-and-cookies aisle. From the third slot I look straight
up this aisle to the meat counter, and I watched them all the
way. The fat one with the tan sort of fumbled with the

cookies, but on second thought she put the package back. The sheep pushing their carts down the aisle—the girls were walking against the usual traffic (not that we have one-way signs or anything)—were pretty hilarious. You could see them, when Queenie's white shoulders dawned on them, kind of jerk, or hop, or hiccup, but their eyes snapped back to their own baskets and on they pushed. I bet you could set off dynamite in an A & P and the people would by and large keep reaching and checking oatmeal off their lists and muttering "Let me see, there was a third thing, began with A, asparagus, no, ah, yes, applesauce!" or whatever it is they do mutter. But there was no doubt, this jiggled them. A few houseslaves in pin curlers even looked around after pushing their carts past to make sure what they had seen was correct.

You know, it's one thing to have a girl in a bathing suit down on the beach, where what with the glare nobody can look at each other much anyway, and another thing in the cool of the A & P, under the fluorescent lights, against all those stacked packages, with her feet paddling along naked over our checkerboard green-and-cream rubber-tile floor.

"Oh Daddy," Stokesie said beside me. "I feel so faint."

"Darling," I said. "Hold me tight." Stokesie's married, with two babies chalked up on his fuselage already, but as far as I can tell that's the only difference. He's twenty-two, and I was nineteen this April.

"Is it done?" he asks, the responsible married man finding his voice. I forgot to say he thinks he's going to be manager some sunny day, maybe in 1990 when it's called the Great Alexandrov and Petrooshki Tea Company or something.

What he meant was, our town is five miles from a beach, with a big summer colony out on the Point, but we're right in the middle of town, and the women generally put on a shirt or shorts or something before they get out of the car into the street. And anyway these are usually women with six children and varicose veins mapping their legs and nobody, including them, could care less. As I say, we're right in the middle of town, and if you stand at our front doors you can see two banks and the Congregational church and the newspaper store and three real-estate offices and about twenty-seven old freeloaders tearing up Central Street because the sewer broke again. It's not as if we're on the Cape; we're north of Boston and there's people in this town haven't seen the ocean for twenty years.

The girls had reached the meat counter and were asking

McMahon something. He pointed, they pointed, and they shuffled out of sight behind a pyramid of Diet Delight peaches. All that was left for us to see was old McMahon patting his mouth and looking after them sizing up their joints. Poor kids, I began to feel sorry for them, they couldn't help it.

Now here comes the sad part of the story, at least my family says it's sad, but I don't think it's so sad myself. The store's pretty empty, it being Thursday afternoon, so there was nothing much to do except lean on the register and wait for the girls to show up again. The whole store was like a pinball machine and I didn't know which tunnel they'd come out of. After a while they come around out of the far aisle, around the light bulbs, records at discount of the Caribbean Six or Tony Martin Sings or some such gunk you wonder they waste the wax on, sixpacks of candy bars, and plastic toys done up in cellophane that fall apart when a kid looks at them anyway. Around they come, Queenie still leading the way, and holding a little gray jar in her hand. Slots Three through Seven are unmanned and I could see her wondering between Stokes and me, but Stokesie with his usual luck draws an old party in baggy gray pants who stumbles up with four giant cans of pineapple juice (what do these bums *do* with all that pineapple juice? I've often asked myself) so the girls come to me. Queenie puts down the jar and I take it into my fingers icy cold. Kingfish Fancy Herring Snacks in Pure Sour Cream: 49¢. Now her hands are empty, not a ring or a bracelet, bare as God made them, and I wonder where the money's coming from. Still with that prim look she lifts a folded dollar bill out of the hollow at the center of her nubbled pink top. The jar went heavy in my hand. Really, I thought that was so cute.

Then everybody's luck begins to run out. Lengel comes in from haggling with a truck full of cabbages on the lot and is about to scuttle into that door marked MANAGER behind which he hides all day when the girls touch his eye. Lengel's pretty dreary, teaches Sunday school and the rest, but he doesn't miss that much. He comes over and says, "Girls, this isn't the beach."

Queenie blushes, though maybe it's just a brush of sunburn I was noticing for the first time, now that she was so close. "My mother asked me to pick up a jar of herring snacks." Her voice kind of startled me, the way voices do when you see the people first, coming out so flat and dumb yet kind of tony, too, the way it ticked over "pick up" and "snacks." All of a sudden I slid right down her voice into her living room. Her father and the other men were standing around in ice-cream coats and bow ties and the women were in sandals picking up herring snacks on toothpicks off a big glass plate and they were all holding drinks the color of water with olives and sprigs of mint in them. When my parents have somebody over they get lemonade and if it's a real racy affair Schlitz in tall glasses with "They'll Do It Every Time" cartoons stenciled on.

"That's all right," Lengel said. "But this isn't the beach." His repeating this struck me as funny, as if it had just occurred to him, and he had been thinking all these years the A & P was a great big sand dune and he was the head lifeguard. He didn't like my smiling—as I say he doesn't miss much—but he concentrates on giving the girls that sad Sunday-school-superintendent stare.

Queenie's blush is no sunburn now, and the plump one in plaid, that I liked better from the back—a really sweet can —pipes up, "We weren't doing any shopping. We just came in for the one thing."

"That makes no difference," Lengel tells her, and I could see from the way his eyes went that he hadn't noticed she was wearing a two-piece before. "We want you decently dressed when you come in here."

"We *are* decent," Queenie says suddenly, her lower lip pushing, getting sore now that she remembers her place, a place from which the crowd that runs the A & P must look pretty crummy. Fancy Herring Snacks flashed in her very blue eyes.

"Girls, I don't want to argue with you. After this come in here with your shoulders covered. It's our policy." He turns his back. That's policy for you. Policy is what the kingpins want. What the others want is juvenile delinquency.

All this while, the customers had been showing up with their carts but, you know, sheep, seeing a scene, they had all bunched up on Stokesie, who shook open a paper bag as gently as peeling a peach, not wanting to miss a word. I could feel in the silence everybody getting nervous, most of all Lengel, who asks me, "Sammy, have you rung up their purchase?"

I thought and said "No" but it wasn't about that I was thinking. I go through the punches, 4, 9, GROC, TOT—it's more complicated than you think, and after you do it often enough, it begins to make a little song, that you hear words to, in my

case "Hello (*bing*) there, you (*gung*) hap-py *pee*-pul (*splat*)!"
—the *splat* being the drawer flying out. I uncrease the bill,
tenderly as you may imagine, it just having come from between the two smoothest scoops of vanilla I had ever known
were there, and pass a half and a penny into her narrow pink
palm, and nestle the herrings in a bag and twist its neck and
hand it over, all the time thinking.

The girls, and who'd blame them, are in a hurry to get out,
so I say "I quit" to Lengel quick enough for them to hear,
hoping they'll stop and watch me, their unsuspected hero.
They keep right on going, into the electric eye; the door flies
open and they flicker across the lot to their car, Queenie and
Plaid and Big Tall Goony-Goony (not that as raw material
she was so bad), leaving me with Lengel and a kink in his
eyebrow.

"Did you say something, Sammy?"

"I said I quit."

"I thought you did."

"You didn't have to embarrass them."

"It was they who were embarrassing us."

I started to say something that came out "Fiddle-de-doo."
It's a saying of my grandmother's, and I know she would have
been pleased.

"I don't think you know what you're saying," Lengel said.

"I know you don't," I said. "But I do." I pull the bow at
the back of my apron and start shrugging it off my shoulders.
A couple customers that had been heading for my slot begin
to knock against each other, like scared pigs in a chute.

Lengel sighs and begins to look very patient and old and
gray. He's been a friend of my parents for years. "Sammy,
you don't want to do this to your Mom and Dad," he tells me.
It's true, I don't. But it seems to me that once you begin a
gesture it's fatal not to go through with it. I fold the apron,
"Sammy" stitched in red on the pocket, and put it on the
counter, and drop the bow tie on top of it. The bow tie is
theirs, if you've ever wondered. "You'll feel this for the rest of
your life," Lengel says, and I know that's true, too, but remembering how he made that pretty girl blush makes me so
scrunchy inside I punch the No Sale tab and the machine
whirs "pee-pul" and the drawer splats out. One advantage to
this scene taking place in summer, I can follow this up with
a clean exit, there's no fumbling around getting your coat and
galoshes, I just saunter into the electric eye in my white shirt
that my mother ironed the night before, and the door heaves

itself open, and outside the sunshine is skating around on the asphalt.

I look around for my girls, but they're gone, of course. There wasn't anybody but some young married screaming with her children about some candy they didn't get by the door of a powder-blue Falcon station wagon. Looking back in the big windows, over the bags of peat moss and aluminum lawn furniture stacked on the pavement, I could see Lengel in my place in the slot, checking the sheep through. His face was dark gray and his back stiff, as if he'd just had an injection of iron, and my stomach kind of fell as I felt how hard the world was going to be to me hereafter.

The air was as soft, as kind, as the water; there was no hostility in either. The two elements, as Ralph came out of one into the other, seemed tints of a single enveloping benevolence.

"Oh, yes, but not merely that," the doctor's wife said. "He loved the people. He built them three churches and, oh, did all manner of good works. We're talking of Reverend Johnson," she explained to Eve, who had remained on the beach with the children. "The Anglican padre. He retired last year and went back to England. Sussex, I think."

"He loved the people?" Eve asked. She had heard. Voices carried well in the air, disturbed, during the day, by only the whispering beat of the surf and infrequent voices calling in English made musical by an unintelligible lilt.

The doctor's wife dropped down on the sand. "These are my children," she intoned gruffly. She chased the abrupt parody away with her sharp laughter. "Oh, yes, he loved them. He gave his life to them." The youthful excitement of her voice and the innocent clarity of her eyes went queerly with her body, which was middle-aged. Her plump legs had gone lumpy and sodden, and her small face was finely wrinkled, each wrinkle accented by a line of white where the pinched skin had evaded the sun. "He didn't have any children of his own," she thought to add. "Just this dreadful dog Hooker. Such a funny old man. You might have liked him. I'm sure you never see his kind in America."

"I know we would have liked him," Eve said. "Hannah often mentions Reverend Johnson." Hannah was their cook, a woman of over thirty yet as shy and subtle as a girl. Her skin was always shining as if in embarrassment, but she had a jaunty way of crooning hymns to herself in the kitchen. The children, at first timid of her color, adored her, and listened with eyes rounded by delight when she held up a two-tone forefinger and told them to be good. Goodness had never before been presented to them seriously. Ralph and Eve had not expected a servant. They had picked the most obscure island they could find. But Hannah came with the house; the owner, a svelte widow who had children in Florida, Peru, and Antigua, assumed they would need her. As it turned out, they did. They could never have unravelled alone all the riddles of this novel world. Eve could never have managed the shopping, which was carried on by gossip—invisible voices as liquid as the wind, telling who had just slaughtered a pig, and whose fishing boat had come in with a catch. The village was full of

stores; almost every shack at least sold—for disturbingly dis-
crepant prices—American cigarettes smuggled from St. Martin. But even the business hours of the most official store, a
cement corridor of shelves attached to the customs office, had
proved a mystery the Americans were unable to crack. They
always found barred the large green door bearing in wobbly
chalk script the ancient announcement "Attention Members!
Attention Friends! This Store will be CLOSED Thursday
afternoon."

"Oh, Hannah. She's a good girl," the doctor's wife said,
and rolled over on her stomach. The corrugated backs of her
thighs were frosted with sand like wet sugar.

"She is, you know," Eve said. "She's lovely. I think they're
all lovely. They've all been lovely to us." Such insistence was
unlike his wife. Ralph wondered what was between the two
women, who had just met a day ago. "I can see why Reverend
Johnson loved the people," Eve added in a deliberate, though
cautiously soft, voice. "The people" were all around them;
their huts came down to the edge of the sand, and, windows
shuttered, the patched walls seemed to be listening raptly.

The doctor's wife rolled over again and returned to a sitting
position. What was making her so restless?

"Yes," she said, and an especially heavy curl of surf foamed
up the white slope and soaked in just short of their feet. The
sand was porous; innumerable punctures dotted it, the breath-
ing-holes of crabs. The doctor's wife's eyes fixed on the
horizon and became, from the side, colorless lenses. Her nose
in profile turned acute. "They're simple souls," she said.

The doctor's wife was a queen here. She was the only
fully white woman resident on the island. When the rare
British official and the rarer, fantastically minor member of
royalty came to grace this most remote and docile scrap of
empire with a visit, she was the hostess. When she roared
along the dirt roads in her spattered English Ford—its muffler
had long ago rotted away—the older natives touched their
foreheads ironically and the children flapped their arms in
her wake of dust. When she and the doctor condescended to
call upon the American family staying three weeks in The
Bay, Hannah had trembled with pride and broken a cup in the
kitchen. The doctor was a slight, rapid-voiced man with a
witty air of failure. His fingertips were dyed deep yellow by
smuggled cigarettes. He preferred Camels, but Chesterfields
were all that were coming through now. Camels had more

scratch in them. He had never seen a filtered cigarette. He and his wife had been ten years in the tropics—B.G., Trinidad, Barbados, now this. He had some vague scheme of getting to America and making a fortune and retiring to a Yorkshire village. He was off for the day to St. Martin.

"In America, now," the doctor's wife said, vehemently brushing sand from her knees, "are the coloreds well cared for?"

"How do you mean?" Eve asked.

"Are they well off?"

"Not really," Ralph said, because he sensed that it would be better if he, rather than Eve, answered. "In some parts better than others. In the South, of course, they're openly discriminated against; in the North they by and large have to live in the city slums but at least they have full legal rights."

"Oh, dear," the doctor's wife said. "It is a problem, isn't it?"

Eve's face flashed up from studying a shell. "Whose problem?" she asked. She was a graduate of one of those female colleges where only a member of a racial minority or a cripple can be elected class president. News from South Africa made her voice thrash, and she was for anyone—Castro, Ben-Gurion, Martin Luther King—who in her mind represented an oppressed race. That such automatic sympathy was itself condescending had not occurred to her. Of English blood, enriched by remote and aristocratic injections of French and Russian, she denied the less favored even the compliment of fearing them.

The doctor's wife returned her gaze to the horizon, and Ralph wondered if they had been rude. In the woman's pointed profile there was a certain perhaps deliberately noble thrust. But, the hostess, she relented and tried to make the conversation go again. She turned her head, shading her eyes with a quick hand and exposing her neat white teeth in a tense smile. "The schools," she said. "Can they go to your schools?"

"Of course," Ralph said swiftly, at the same time realizing that for her there was no "of course" to it. She knew nothing about his country. He felt firmer, having gauged her ignorance, and having moved to the hard ground of information. "Nobody denies them schools. In the South the schools are segregated. But in the North, and the West, and so on, there's no problem." He hunched his shoulders, feeling at his back Eve's disapproval of his saying "problem."

"But"—the doctor's wife's freckles gathered under her

eyes as she squinted into the focus of the issue—"would *your* children go to school with them?"

"Sure. Good heavens. Why not?" He was relieved to clear this up, to lock this door. He hoped the doctor's wife would now turn away and talk of something else.

She sighed. "Of course, you in America have lived with the problem so long. In England, now, they're just waking up; the blacks are *pouring* into London."

A wave, pushed by one behind it, slid so far up the slant of sand their feet were delicately shocked and soaked. For a few seconds their ankles glittered in rippling sleeves of retreating water. Eve said slowly, "You talk as if they had asked to be made slaves and brought here."

"Mommy, look! Mommy, look!" Kate's voice, mingling with Larry's babyish yips of excitement, came from far down the beach. Their little silhouettes were jiggling around something dark at their feet, and out of the sea grape an old woman in a kerchief and a young sailor with a naked chest had emerged to watch them, amused to see what amused these strange children. Eve rose, casting down, for Ralph to see, a startled and indignant look at the doctor's wife's body, as if it were an offensive piece of rubbish washed up on the pure sands of her mind.

As Eve walked away, the doctor's wife said, "Doesn't she take a tan beautifully?"

"Yes, she always does. She's part French." With his wife out of earshot, Ralph relaxed into the sand. Mediating between the two women had demanded an exhausting equilibrium. He resigned himself to listening; he knew the doctor's wife's tongue would be loosened. The presence of another white queen inhibited her, diluted her authority.

"Do you want to hear a frightening story?"

"Sure." He acquiesced uneasily. The attention of the houses behind them seemed to grow more intense. He felt that he and his family were liked in the village; the doctor's wife, driving down from the center of the island to enjoy their beach, assumed an incriminating alliance which he did not wish to exist. For when the sun went down, she would go home, leaving them alone in the village with the night and its noises. Their tilly lamps hissed; black bugs droned into their heat and fell crackling to the floor; far up the road a boy practiced on his lonely steel drum and next door, in an unpainted cabin that was never unshuttered, a woman wailed and a man infrequently growled a brief, hurt complaint.

"When Vic Johnson left," the doctor's wife said, lowering her voice and sinking back on her elbow, to bring her face closer to Ralph's, "they had a party to greet the new parson, a very nice young colored boy from St. Kitts. *Very* nice, I must say, and they say very intelligent, though I haven't heard him preach. Well, the Warden—you haven't met him, and I dare say you won't, a big smooth Jamaican, takes himself oh *ever* so seriously—the Warden makes this little speech. He of course mentions Vic, forty years and so on, but right at the end he says that he knows we will not miss Reverend Johnson, because the new vicar is such a fine young man, comes to us with such an excellent record of study, and the rest of it, and furthermore, *furthermore,* what makes us especially happy and proud, he is one of us. Imagine! One of us! Of course, the young parson was embarrassed to death. It made me so mad I would have jumped up and left if the doctor hadn't held my hand. *One of us!* Vic had given his life to these people."

Her voice had become shrill; Ralph spoke in the hope of restraining it. "It seems unnecessary; but natural," he said.

"I don't see anything natural about it. *Un*natural, in my book. Unnatural, childish ingratitude. You just don't know how unnatural these people are. If you could see one-tenth of the antics, and then the selfishness, the doctor puts up with. At two in the morning, 'Doctor, Doctor, come save my child,' and then a week later, when he tries to collect his poor little dollar or two, they don't *remember.* They don't remember at all. And if he insists—'The white people are stealing our money.' Oh. I hate them. God forgive me, I've come to hate them. They're *not* natural. They're not fully human." Seeing his hand begin a protesting movement, she added, "And for that matter, do you know what they say about you and your wife?" It was as if a shadow cruising through her words now made its lunge.

"No. Do they say something?"

"This is just to show how malicious they are. They say your wife has a touch of the brush." It took Ralph a moment to expand "brush" into "tarbrush." He laughed; what else?

The doctor's wife laughed, too; but under the blond eyebrows her blue eyes, the pupils pinpricks in the sun, were fixed on his face. She expected his face to crack and the truth to escape. "You see how dark she is," she explained. "How tan." He watched her tongue tick as she suspensefully pronounced the last two words. Girlish curiosity gave a taut surface to her mature malice.

Blood rushed through his body; the wound was confused; his anger entangled him with his attacker. He was supplying an absurd assault with teeth out of himself. "She just naturally gets that brown."

"And you see," the doctor's wife went on, still not unpinning her eyes from his face, "that's why they say you came here. No tourists come here, least of all with children. They say your wife's being part Negro has kept you out of the hotels on the better islands."

He felt certain that this ingenious argument was wholly her own. "We came here because it was cheap," he said.

"Of *course*," she said, "of *course*," and giggled, sensing that she had exposed herself to his defense. "But they can't believe that. They believe, you see, that all Americans are *rich*." Which was just what, Ralph knew, she and the doctor believed.

He stood up, wet sand collapsing from his legs. In an effort to rein his excitement, he threw several unrelated laughs, as if out of a renewed apprehension of absurdity, outward into the air. He looked down at the woman and said, "Well, that explains why they seem to like her better than me."

The doctor's wife, having strained her neck to squint up at him, collapsed the rest of the way. She pillowed her head with one arm and threw the other over her eyes. Without her eyes her lips seemed vague and numb. "Oh, no," she said. "They hate her for getting away with it."

His laughter this time was totally vacant; it humiliated him. "I think I'll go in again," he said. "Before the sun fades."

"It won't fade," was the faint answer.

From the safety of the water he watched his dark wife herd his two pale, burned children up the beach. The distance between them and the doctor's wife's inert body diminished; he had an urge to shout a warning, then smiled, picturing the laughter that would greet this story when they were home, at a cocktail party, secure among their own. Abruptly, he felt guilty in relation to his wife. He had betrayed her. His seriousness had been unworthy of her. She would have wanted him to say yes, her grandfather picked cotton in Alabama, in America these things are taken for granted, we have no problem. But he saw, like something living glimpsed in a liquid volume, that the comedy of this response depended upon, could only live within, a vast unconscious pride of race. That since this medium was poisoned all its creatures must be evil. That he and the doctor's wife were immersed together; he hated her blue eyes because they were pinned to his face, hated the taste of her because—could it be?—she was dying. His guilt could not be mapped. Its intricacy was as dense as a simple mass. He moved backward in the ocean, touching the ribbed bottom with his toes, until the water wrapped around his throat. Something—seaweed or the pulse of a current—touched his calf. He thrashed, and peered down, but saw nothing. He was afraid of the sharks, and he was afraid of the doctor's wife, so he hung there between them, bleeding shame, while the water forgave him.

Lifeguard

BEYOND DOUBT, I am a splendid fellow. In the autumn, winter, and spring, I execute the duties of a student of divinity; in the summer I disguise myself in my skin and become a lifeguard. My slightly narrow and gingerly hirsute but not necessarily unmanly chest becomes brown. My smooth back turns the color of caramel, which, in conjunction with the whipped cream of my white pith helmet, gives me, some of my teen-age satellites assure me, a delightfully edible appearance. My legs, which I myself can study, cocked as they are before me while I repose on my elevated wooden throne, are dyed a lustreless maple walnut that accentuates their articulate strength. Correspondingly, the hairs of my body are bleached blond, so that my legs have the pointed elegance of, within the flower, umber anthers dusted with pollen.

For nine months of the year, I pace my pale hands and burning eyes through immense pages of Biblical text barnacled with fudging commentary; through multivolumed apologetics couched in a falsely friendly Victorian voice and bound in subtly abrasive boards of finely ridged, prefaded red; through handbooks of liturgy and histories of dogma; through the bewildering duplicities of Tillich's divine politicking; through the suave table talk of Father D'Arcy, Etienne Gilson, Jacques Maritain, and other such moderns mistakenly put at their ease by the exquisite antique furniture and overstuffed larder of the hospitable St. Thomas; through the terrifying attempts of Kierkegaard, Berdyaev, and Barth to scourge God into being. I sway appalled on the ladder of minus signs by which theologians would surmount the void. I tiptoe like a burglar into the house of naturalism to steal the silver. An acrobat, I swing from wisp to wisp. Newman's iridescent cobwebs crush in my hands. Pascal's blackboard mathematics are erased by a passing shoulder. The cave drawings, astoundingly vital by candlelight, of those aboriginal magicians, Paul and Augustine, in daylight fade into mere anthropology. The diverting productions of literary flirts like Chesterton, Eliot, Auden, and Greene—whether they regard Christianity as a pastel forest designed for a fairyland romp or a deliciously miasmic pit from which chiaroscuro can be mined with mechanical buckets—in the end all infallibly strike, despite the comic variety of gongs and mallets, the note of the rich young man who on the coast of Judaea refused in dismay to sell all that he had.

Then, for the remaining quarter of the solar revolution, I rest my eyes on a sheet of brilliant sand printed with the runes of naked human bodies. That there is no discrepancy between my studies, that the texts of the flesh complement those of the mind, is the easy burden of my sermon.

On the back rest of my lifeguard's chair is painted a cross—true, a red cross, signifying bandages, splints, spirits of ammonia, and sunburn unguents. Nevertheless, it comforts me. Each morning, as I mount into my chair, my athletic and youthfully fuzzy toes expertly gripping the slats that make a ladder, it is as if I am climbing into an immense, rigid, loosely fitting vestment.

Again, in each of my roles I sit attentively perched on the edge of an immensity. That the sea, with its multiform and mysterious hosts, its savage and senseless rages, no longer comfortably serves as a divine metaphor indicates how severely humanism has corrupted the apples of our creed. We seek God now in flowers and good deeds, and the immensities of blue that surround the little scabs of land upon which we draw our lives to their unsatisfactory conclusions are suffused by science with vacuous horror. I myself can hardly bear the thought of stars, or begin to count the mortalities of coral. But from my chair the sea, slightly distended by my higher perspective, seems a misty old gentleman stretched at his ease in an immense armchair which has for arms the arms of this bay and for an antimacassar the freshly laundered sky. Sailboats float on his surface like idle and unrelated but benevolent thoughts. The soughing of the surf is the rhythmic lifting of his ripple-stitched vest as he breathes. Consider. We enter the sea with a shock; our skin and blood shout in protest. But, that instant, that leap, past, what do we find? Ecstasy and buoyance. Swimming offers a parable. We struggle and thrash, and drown; we succumb, even in despair, and float, and are saved.

With what timidity, with what a sense of trespass, do I set forward even this obliquely a thought so official! Forgive me. I am not yet ordained; I am too disordered to deal with the main text. My competence is marginal, and I will confine myself to the gloss of flesh with which this particular margin, this one beach, is annotated each day.

Here the cinema of life is run backwards. The old are the first to arrive. They are idle, and have lost the gift of sleep. Each of our bodies is a clock that loses time. Young as I am, I can hear in myself the protein acids ticking; I wake at odd hours and in the shuddering darkness and silence feel my death rushing toward me like an express train. The older we get, and the fewer the mornings left to us, the more deeply dawn stabs us awake. The old ladies wear wide straw hats and, in their hats' shadows, smiles as wide, which they bestow upon each other, upon salty shells they discover in the morning-smooth sand, and even upon me, downy-eyed from my night of dissipation. The gentlemen are often incongruous; withered white legs support brazen barrel chests, absurdly potent, bustling with white froth. How these old roosters preen on their "condition"! With what fatuous expertness they swim in the icy water—always, however, prudently parallel to the shore, at a depth no greater than their height.

Then come the middle-aged, burdened with children and aluminum chairs. The men are scarred with the marks of their vocation—the red forearms of the gasoline-station attendant, the pale X on the back of the overall-wearing mason or carpenter, the clammer's nicked ankles. The hair on their bodies has as many patterns as matted grass. The women are wrinkled but fertile, like the Iraqi rivers that cradled the seeds of our civilization. Their children are odious. From their gaunt faces leer all the vices, the greeds, the grating urgencies of the adult, unsoftened by maturity's reticence and fatigue. Except that here and there, a girl, the eldest daughter, wearing a knit suit striped horizontally with green, purple, and brown, walks slowly, carefully, puzzled by the dawn enveloping her thick smooth body, her waist not yet nipped but her throat elongated.

Finally come the young. The young matrons bring fat and fussing infants who gobble the sand like sugar, who toddle blissfully into the surf and bring me bolt upright on my throne. My whistle tweets. The mothers rouse. Many of these women are pregnant again, and sluggishly lie in their loose suits like cows tranced in a meadow. They gossip politics, and smoke incessantly, and lift their troubled eyes in wonder as a trio of flat-stomached nymphs parades past. These maidens take all our eyes. The vivacious redhead, freckled and white-footed, pushing against her boy and begging to be ducked; the solemn brunette, transporting the vase of herself with held breath; the dimpled blonde in the bib and diapers of her Bikini, the lambent fuzz of her midriff shimmering like a cat's belly. Lust stuns me like the sun.

You are offended that a divinity student lusts? What prigs the unchurched are. Are not our assaults on the supernatural lascivious, a kind of indecency? If only you knew what de Sadian degradations, what frightful psychological spelunking, our gentle transcendentalist professors set us to, as preparation for our work, which is to shine in the darkness.

I feel that my lust makes me glow; I grow cold in my chair, like a torch of ice, as I study beauty. I have studied much of it, wearing all styles of bathing suit and facial expression, and have come to this conclusion: a woman's beauty lies, not in any exaggeration of the specialized zones, nor in any general harmony that could be worked out by means of the *sectio aurea* or a similar aesthetic superstition; but in the arabesque of the spine. The curve by which the back modulates into the buttocks. It is here that grace sits and rides a woman's body.

I watch from my white throne and pity women, deplore the demented judgment that drives them toward the braggart muscularity of the mesomorph and the prosperous complacence of the endomorph when it is we ectomorphs who pack in our scrawny sinews and exacerbated nerves the most intense gift, the most generous shelter, of love. To desire a woman is to desire to save her. Anyone who has endured intercourse that was neither predatory nor hurried knows how through it we descend, with a partner, into the grotesque and delicate shadows that until then have remained locked in the most guarded recess of our soul: into this harbor we bring her. A vague and twisted terrain becomes inhabited; each shadow, touched by the exploration, blooms into a flower of act. As if we are an island upon which a woman, tossed by her laboring vanity and blind self-seeking, is blown, and there finds security, until, an instant before the anticlimax, Nature with a smile thumps down her trump, and the island sinks beneath the sea.

There is great truth in those motion pictures which are

slandered as true neither to the Bible nor to life. They are—
written though they are by demons and drunks—true to both.
We are all Solomons lusting for Sheba's salvation. The God-
filled man is filled with a wilderness that cries to be populated.
The stony chambers need jewels, furs, tints of cloth and flesh,
even though, as in Samson's case, the temple comes tumbling.
Women are an alien race of pagans set down among us.
Every seduction is a conversion.

Who has loved and not experienced that sense of rescue?
It is not true that our biological impulses are tricked out with
ribands of chivalry; rather, our chivalric impulses go clanking
in encumbering biological armor. Eunuchs love. Children
love. I would love.

My chief exercise, as I sit above the crowds, is to lift the
whole mass into immortality. It is not a light task; the throng
is so huge, and its members so individually unworthy. No
memento mori is so clinching as a photograph of a vanished
crowd. Cheering Roosevelt, celebrating the Armistice, there
it is, wearing its ten thousand straw hats and stiff collars, a
fearless and wooden-faced bustle of life: it is gone. A crowd
dies in the street like a derelict; it leaves no heir, no trace, no
name. My own persistence beyond the last rim of time is
easy to imagine; indeed, the effort of imagination lies the other
way—to conceive of my ceasing. But when I study the vast
tangle of humanity that blackens the beach as far as the sand
stretches, absurdities crowd in on me. Is it as maiden, matron,
or crone that the females will be eternalized? What will they
do without children to watch and gossip to exchange? What
of the thousand deaths of memory and bodily change we en-
dure—can each be redeemed at a final Adjustments Counter?
The sheer numbers involved make the mind scream. The race
is no longer a tiny clan of simian aristocrats lording it over an
ocean of grass; mankind is a plague racing like fire across
the exhausted continents. This immense clot gathered on the
beach, a fraction of a fraction—can we not say that this
breeding swarm is its own immortality and end the suspense?
The beehive in a sense survives; and is each of us not proved
to be a hive, a galaxy of cells each of whom is doubtless pray-
ing, from its pew in our thumbnail or esophagus, for personal
resurrection? Indeed, to the cells themselves cancer may seem
a revival of faith. No, in relation to other people oblivion is
sensible and sanitary.

This sea of others exasperates and fatigues me most on
Sunday mornings. I don't know why people no longer go to

church—whether they have lost the ability to sing or the willingness to listen. From eight-thirty onward they crowd in from the parking lots, ants each carrying its crumb of baggage, until by noon, when the remote churches are releasing their gallant and gaily dressed minority, the sea itself is jammed with hollow heads and thrashing arms like a great bobbing backwash of rubbish. A transistor radio somewhere in the sand releases in a thin, apologetic gust the closing peal of a transcribed service. And right here, here at the very height of torpor and confusion, I slump, my eyes slit, and the blurred forms of Protestantism's errant herd seem gathered by the water's edge in impassioned poses of devotion. I seem to be lying dreaming in the infinite rock of space before Creation, and the actual scene I see is a vision of impossibility: a Paradise. For had we existed before the gesture that split the firmament, could we have conceived of our most obvious possession, our most platitudinous blessing, the moment, the single ever-present moment that we perpetually bring to our lips brimful?

So: be joyful. Be Joyful in my commandment. It is the message I read in your jiggle. Stretch your skins like pegged hides curing in the miracle of the sun's moment. Exult in your legs' scissoring, your waist's swivel. Romp; eat the froth; be children. I am here above you; I have given my youth that you may do this. I wait. The tides of time have treacherous undercurrents. You are borne continually toward the horizon. I have prepared myself; my muscles are instilled with everything that must be done. Someday my alertness will bear fruit; from near the horizon there will arise, delicious, translucent, like a green bell above the water, the call for help, the call, a call, it saddens me to confess, that I have yet to hear.

The Crow In The Woods

ALL THE WARM NIGHT the secret snow fell so adhesively that
every twig in the woods about their little rented house supported a tall slice of white, an upward projection which in
the shadowless glow of early morning lifted depth from the
scene, made it seem Chinese, calligraphic, a stiff tapestry hung
from the gray sky, a shield of lace interwoven with black
thread. Jack wondered if he had ever seen anything so beautiful before. The snow had stopped. As if it had been a func-
tion of his sleep.

He was standing in his bathrobe by the window at dawn
because last evening, amid an intricate and antique luxury,
he and his wife had dined with their landlords. Two wines,
red and darker red, had come with the dinner. Candles on the
long table. Two other couples, older, subtly ravaged. Dinner
over, the men and women separated and then, the men's
throats rasped by brandy and cigars, rejoined in a large room
whose walls were, astoundingly, green silk. The mixed sexes
chattered immersed in an incoherent brilliance like chandelier
facets clashing. And at the end (the clock on the gray marble
mantel stating the precipitate hour with golden hands whose
threadlike fineness seemed itself a kind of pointed tact) in a
final and desperate-feeling flight all swooped up the curving
stairs and by invitation into the chamber where in daytime
hours the white-haired hostess conducted her marvellous
hobby of *cartonnage*. She had fashioned a pagoda of cut
colored papers. On the walls there were paper bouquets of
flowers framed. On the worktable the most immense, the most
triumphantly glossy and nozzled bottle of Elmer's Glue Jack
had ever seen; he had never dreamed such a size could exist.
The blue bull impressed on the bottle jubilantly laughed. Serv-
ants came and wrapped their coats around them. On the front
porch the departing guests discovered at midnight a world

152

thinly disguised in snow. The universal descent of snow restricted the area of their vision; outdoors had a domed intimacy. The guests carolled praise; the host, a short and old man, arthritic, preened: his dinner, his wine, his wife's *cartonnage,* and now his snow. Looped, the young couple returned to the little rented house that even was his. They satisfied the sitter, dismissed her into the storm like a disgrace, and, late as it was, made love. So in a reflex of gratitude, when six hours later their child cried, the man arose instead of his wife, and administered comfort.

The soaked diaper released an invisible cloud of ammonia that washed tears into his eyes. The whiteness edging the windows made decisive and cutting the light of the sun, burning behind the sky like a bulb in a paper lampshade. The child's room had become incandescent; the wallpaper, flowered with pale violets, glowed evenly, so that even the fluff-cluttered corners brimmed with purity.

The wordless girl, stripped and puzzled, studied the usual figure of her father, out of season at this hour. The purple bathrobe's wool embrace and the cold pressure of the floor on his feet alike felt flattering; magnified him. His naked giant's thighs kept thrusting between the leaves of the bathrobe into the white air. He saw them, saw everything, through three polished sheets of glass: the memory of his drunkenness, his present insufficiency of sleep, and the infiltrating brilliance of the circumambient snow. As his impressions were sharp, so he was soft. The parallel floorcracks, the paint's salmon sheen, his daughter's sombre and intent gaze like the gaze of a chemically distended pupil—these things received through an instrument which fatigue had wiped clean of distractions, bit deeply into him and pressed, with an urgency not disagreeable, on his bowels.

Though the house was small, it had two bathrooms. He used the one attached to his daughter's room, where the square shower-curtain rod wobbled and tipped from the repeated weight of wet diapers. Around its bolted root the ceiling plaster had crumbled. He stood under a small shadow of amazement looking down at the oval of still water in which floated his several feces like short rotten sticks, strangely burnished.

The toilet flushed; the whole illuminated interior of the little house seemed purged into action. He dressed his daughter's tumblesome body deftly and carried her to the stairs. The top landing gave on the door to his bedroom; he looked

in and saw that his wife had changed position in the broadened bed. Her naked arms were flung out of the covers and
rested, crook'd, each to a pillow, like spotted ivory framing
the cameo of her averted, maned skull. One breast, lifted by
the twist of her shoulders, shallow in her sleep, was with its
budded center exposed. The sun, probing the shredding sky,
sent low through the woods and windowpanes a diluted fili-
gree, finer than color, that spread across her and up the
swarthy oak headboard a rhomboidal web. Like moths alight-
ing on gauze, her blue eyes opened.

Discovered, he hid downstairs. The child absentmindedly
patted the back of his neck as they descended the tricky narrow steps. These weak touches made his interior tremble as if
with tentative sunshine. Downstairs was darker. The reflection
of the snow was absorbed by the dank and porous furniture.
Rented. Good morning, Mr. Thermostat. The milkman would
be late today: chains slogging a tune on his stout tires: glory
be. The childbearing arm of him ached.

He was unable to find the box of child's cereal. The cup-
boards brimmed with fine sugar and plastic spoons sprawling
in polychrome fans. The catch of the tray of the high chair
snagged; the girl's legs were hinged the wrong way. With
multiplying motions of uncertainty he set water to heating in
a cold-handled pan. Winter. Warm cereal. Where? The ceiling
rumbled; the plumbing sang.

Came the wife and mother, came, wrapped in a blue
cocoon that made her body shapeless, her face white. She had
not been able to go back to sleep after he had left the bed.
Proud, relieved, soft, he sat at the small pine table burnished
with linseed oil. Gerber's wheat-dust came to smoke in the
child's tray. Orange juice, slender as a crayon, was conjured
before him. Like her sister the earth, the woman puts forth
easy flowers of abundance. As he lifted the glass to his lips
he smelled her on his fingertips.

And now released to return to his companion through the
window, he again stared. The woods at their distance across
the frosted lawn were a Chinese screen in which an immense
alphabet of twigs lay hushed: a black robe crusted with white
braid standing of its own stiffness. Nothing in it stirred. There
was no depth, the sky a pearl slab, the woods a fabric of
vision in which vases, arches, and fountains were hushed.

His wife set before him a boiled egg smashed and running
on a piece of toast on a pink plate chipped and gleaming on

the oblique placemat of sunlight flecked with the window-pane's imperfections.

Something happened. Outdoors a huge black bird came flapping with a crow's laborious wingbeat. It banked and, tilted to fit its feet, fell toward the woods. His heart halted in alarm for the crow, with such recklessness assaulting an inviolable surface, seeking so blindly a niche for its strenuous bulk where there was no depth. It could not enter. Its black shape shattering like an instant of flak, the crow plopped into a high branch and sent snow showering from a quadrant of lace. Its wings spread and settled. The vision destroyed, his heart overflowed. "Clare!" he cried.

The woman's pragmatic blue eyes flicked from his face to the window where she saw only snow and rested on the forgotten food steaming between his hands. Her lips moved:

"Eat your egg."

The Blessed Man of Boston, My Grandmother's Thimble, and Fanning Island

I SAW HIM only for a moment, and that was years ago. Boston had been beaten by the White Sox. It was a night game, and when it was over, as the crowd, including myself and my friends, pushed with that suppressed Occidental panic up the aisles toward the exit ramps, he, like the heavy pebble of gold that is not washed from the pan, was revealed, sitting alone, immobile and smiling, among the green seats. He was an old Chinese man, solidly fat, like a Chevrolet dealer, and he wore faded black trousers and a white shirt whose sleeves were rolled up. He sat with one arm up on the back of the seat beside him and smiled out toward the field, where the ground crew was unfurling the tarp across the foreshortened clay diamond and the outfield under the arc lights looked as brilliant and flat as a pool-table felt. And it flashed upon me, as I glimpsed this man sitting alone and unperturbed among the drained seats, that here was the happy man, the man of unceasing and effortless blessing. I thought then to write a novel, an immense book, about him, recounting his every move, his every meal, every play, pitch, and hesitation of every ball game he attended, the number of every house he passed as he walked Boston's Indian-colored slums, the exact position and shape of every cracked and flaking spot on the doorways, the precise scumble and glitter of every floriate and convoluted fancy of ironwork that drifted by his legs, the chalk-marks, the bricks (purple-tinted, ochre-smeared, red), the constellations of lint and stain in his tiny bachelor's room (green walls, painted pipes coughing with steam, telephone wiring stapled along the baseboard), the never-precisely-

156

duplicated curl of the smoke off his rice, the strokes of sound composing the hatchings of noise at his back, every stifled cry, every sizzle of a defective neon sign connection, every distant plane and train, every roller-skate scratch, everything: all set sequentially down with the bald simplicity of intrinsic blessing, thousands upon thousands of pages; ecstatically un-eventful; divinely and defiantly dull.

But we would-be novelists have a reach as shallow as our skins. We walk through volumes of the unexpressed and like snails leave behind a faint thread excreted out of ourselves. From the dew of the few flakes that melt on our faces we cannot reconstruct the snowstorm.

The other night I stumbled downstairs in the dark and kicked my wife's sewing basket from the halfway landing. Needles, spools, buttons, and patches scattered. In gathering the things up, I came upon my grandmother's thimble. For a second I did not know what it was; a stemless chalice of silver weighing a fraction of an ounce had come into my fingers. Then I knew, and the valves of time parted, and after an interval of years my grandmother was upon me again, and it seemed incumbent upon me, necessary and holy, to tell how once there had been a woman who now was no more, how she had been born and lived in a world that had ceased to exist, though its mementos were all about us; how her thimble had been fashioned as if in a magical grotto in the black mountain of time, by workmen dwarfed by remoteness, in a vanished workshop now no larger than the thimble itself and like it soon doomed, as if by geological pressures, to be crushed out of shape. O Lord, bless these poor paragraphs, that would do in their vile ignorance Your work of resurrection.

The thimble was her wedding present to me and my wife. I was her only grandchild. At the time I was married, she was in her late seventies, crippled and enfeebled. She had fought a long battle with Parkinson's disease; in my earliest mem-ories of her she is touched with it. Her fingers and back are bent; there is a tremble about her as she moves about through the dark, odd-shaped rooms of our house in the town where I was born. Crouched in the hall outside my grandparents' room—which I never entered—I can hear her voice, in a whispering mutter that pierces the wall with little snapping stabs, irritably answer a question that my grandfather had asked inaudibly. It is strange; out of their room, he speaks loudest. When she bends over me, I smell a mixture of must, something like cough medicine, and old cloth permeated with dried sunlight. In my childhood she was strong, endowed with possessions and resources. By the time I married, she had become so weak only her piercing will carried her up and down the stairs of the little country house to which we had moved—the very house where she had lived as a bride. She spoke with great difficulty; she would hang impaled in the middle of a sentence, at a loss for the word, her watery eyes and wild white hair transfixed. She had no possessions. Except for her clothes and her bed, the elegant silver thimble—a gift from her father, inscribed with her maiden initials—was her last property, and she gave it to us.

In those days each departure from her I thought was the last. When I left to be married, I did not expect to see her alive again. But when, at the end of the summer, my wife and I returned, it was my grandfather, and not she, who had died. He had died minutes before we arrived. His body lay on the floor of their bedroom, his mouth a small black triangle in a face withered beyond recognition. The room was dimly lit by the warm glow of a kerosene lamp. I was afraid of his body; it surprised me that she did not seem to be. I was afraid that his body would move. I called "Grandpa" in an experimental whisper and flinched in fear of an answer.

My grandmother sat on the edge of the bed, dazed, smiling slightly to greet me. She was confused, like a craftsman who looks up after a long period of concentration. The sanest of old men, my grandfather had on his last day lost his mind. He had bellowed; she had struggled to restrain him. He thought the bed was on fire and sprang from it; she clung to him and in their fall to the floor he died. But not quite. My mother rushed up the stairs and cried, "What are you doing?"

"Why, we're on the floor," her father told her with level sarcasm, and his heart stopped.

My father met our headlights on the lawn; he was panting. "Jesus," he said to me, "you've come at a funny time; we think Pop's died." My parents-in-law were with us; my wife's father, a surgeon, an intimate of death, went upstairs to the body. He came down, smiling, and said that there was no pulse, though the wrist was still warm. Then when I went upstairs I saw my grandmother smiling in much the same abstracted, considerate way.

She sat, worn and cleansed by her struggle, on the edge of the bed with two hollows. She was a little woman informed by a disproportionate strength. Carrying her husband through his death had been her last great effort. From that moment on, her will tried to arrange itself for defeat, and its power of resistance became an inconvenience to her. I hugged her quickly, afraid of even her body, which had so lately embraced the one on the floor. My mother, behind me, asked her if she wanted to come downstairs with the others. My grandmother refused, saying, "A little while yet," and making a tremulous impatient motion of explanation or dismissal.

She knew, perhaps, what I was shocked to discover when, descending the steps with trembling knees, and tingling all over as if from a bath, I went downstairs: that we have no gestures adequate to answer the imperious gestures of nature. Among deaf mountains human life pursues a comic low road. The sherry that my mother had purchased toward our arrival was served; the wait for the undertaker became overlaid with a subdued version of the party she had meant to have. My father-in-law with a chilling professional *finesse* carved the cold ham; my mother, tautly calm, as if at the center of contradictory tensions, made one or two of her witticisms; my father's telephone conversation with our Lutheran minister was as bewildered and bewildering as his conversations with this young man always were. Without knowing what I had expected instead, I was amazed; the chatter seemed to become unbearably loud and I blurted, thinking of my grandmother listening above our heads, "Why can't you let the old man rest?" My mother looked at me in startled reproval, and I felt again the security of being her clever but inexperienced boy; there were things I didn't understand.

The minister came with a drawn white face that cracked in relief at finding laughter in the house. At church softball he had broken his ankle sliding into second base, and limped still. His prayers seemed to chip pieces from our hearts and float them away. The undertaker's men, droll wooden figures like the hangmen of old, came and trundled the body out the door. Thus, as if through a series of pressure locks, we were rescued from the tunnel of death.

My grandmother did not attend the funeral. She was wise, for the Masons made it ridiculous with their occult presumption. My grandmother, whose love of activity had been intense, stayed inside the house, and more and more in bed. When my wife and I went away again—I had a year of college left—I said goodbye to her in my heart. But when we returned at Christmas, she was alive, and she was alive in June, though by now completely bedridden.

Blindly her will gave battle. My grandfather had been a

vigorous booster of exercise as the key to longevity. Obeying, perhaps, an echo of her husband's voice, my grandmother would ask to be lifted by her hands into a sitting position, and then lowered, and lifted again, until the person doing it for her lost patience and in exasperation quit. She liked company, though almost all power of speech had forsaken her. "Up. Up," that fierce and plaintive request, was all I could understand. We knew that the disease touched only her tongue; that in that wordless, glaring head the same alert and appetitive mind lived. But a mind shorn of agency ceases to exist in our world, and we would speak together in her room as if it were empty. Certain, now, that this was my last time with her—my wife and I were going to England for a year—I spent some summer afternoons in my grandmother's room. I knew she could hear, but we had never spoken much to each other, so I would read or write in silence. I remember sitting in the rocking chair at the foot of the bed, near the spot where my grandfather's body had lain that night in warm lamplight, and writing, while the sun streamed in through the geraniums on the window sill, a piece of light verse about what I imagined the sea voyage I was soon to take would be like.

> That line is the horizon line.
> The blue above it is divine.
> The blue below it is marine.
> Sometimes the blue below is green.

Reading this stanza now, I see, as if over the edge of the paper, my grandmother's nostrils as her head was sunk foreshortened in the pillow. The withering force pressed unevenly on her body, twisted it out of symmetry; one nostril was squeezed into teardrop-shape, and the other was a round black hole through which she seemed to seize the air. The whole delicate frame of her existence seemed suspended from this final hungry aperture, the size of a dime, through which her life was sustained.

In England I hesitated to tear open each letter from home, for fear it would contain the news of her death. But, as if preserved in the unreality of those days that passed without weight on a remote continent whose afternoon was our morning and whose morning was our night, she survived, and was there when we returned. We had had a baby girl. We put the child, too young to creep, on my grandmother's bed beside the hump of her legs, so that for an interval four generations were gathered in one room, and without moving her head my grandmother could see her entire progeny: my mother, myself, and my daughter. At her funeral, my child, by then alive to things around her, smiled and from my arms stretched her hand toward the drained and painted body in the casket, perhaps in some faint way familiar.

My grandmother had died, finally, when I was far away, in Boston. I was at a party; it was a Saturday night. I went to the phone with a cigarette in my hand and Cointreau on my breath; my mother, her voice miniature with distance, began the conversation with the two words, "Grammy went." They had found her dead in the morning and had not been able to reach me until now. It was, of course, a blessing; my mother's health had been nearly broken by nursing her. Now we were all released. I returned to the party and told my news, which was received respectfully; it was a small party, of friends. But gaiety cannot be suppressed a whole evening, and when it revived I suppose I joined it. I vowed, groping for some fitness, for the commensurate gesture, to go to a Lutheran church the next morning. But when Sunday morning came, I slept late, and the vow seemed a troublesome whim, I did not go.

I did not go. This refusal seems to be a face at that party and I am about to quarrel with it, but other memories come and touch my elbow and lead me away.

When we were all still alive, the five of us in that kerosene-lit house, on Friday and Saturday nights, at an hour when in the spring and summer there was still abundant light in the air, I would set out in my father's car for town, where my friends lived. I had, by moving ten miles away, at last acquired friends: an illustration of that strange law whereby, like Orpheus leading Eurydice, we achieve our desire by turning our back on it. I had even gained a girl, so that the vibrations were as sexual as social that made me jangle with anticipation as I clowned in front of the mirror in our kitchen, shaving from a basin of stove-heated water, combing my hair with a dripping comb, adjusting my reflection in the mirror until I had achieved just that electric angle from which my face seemed beautiful and everlastingly, by the very volumes of air and sky and grass that lay mutely banked about our home, beloved. My grandmother would hover near me, watching fearfully, as she had when I was a child, afraid that I would fall from a tree. Delirious, humming, I would swoop and lift her, lift her like a child, crooking one arm under her knees and cupping the other behind her back. Exultant in my height, my strength, I would lift that frail brittle body weighing perhaps a hundred pounds and twirl with it in my arms while the rest of the family watched with startled smiles of alarm. Had I stumbled, or dropped her, I might have broken her back, but my joy always proved a secure cradle. And whatever irony was in the impulse, whatever implicit contrast between this ancient husk, scarcely female, and the pliant, warm girl I would embrace before the evening was done, direct delight flooded away: I was carrying her who had carried me, I was giving my past a dance, I had lifted the anxious caretaker of my childhood from the floor, I was bringing her with my boldness to the edge of danger, from which she had always sought to guard me.

There is a photograph of my grandmother and me at the side of the first house. There is snow on the ground. The brick walk has been cleared. I am in a snowsuit, and its bulk makes my walking doubly clumsy. We are both of us dark against the snow and the white brick wall of the house. I am unsteady; my grandmother's black shape bends over me with a predatory solicitude, holding one of my hands in a hand that has already become, under the metamorphosis of her disease, a little clawlike. She was worried that I would fall, that I would not eat enough, that the bigger boys of the neighborhood would harm me, that a cold would strangle me; and her fears were not foolish. There *was* danger in that kind house. Tigers of temper lurked beneath the furniture, and shadows of despair followed my father to the door and flattened themselves against the windows as he walked down the shaded street alone.

I remember watching my mother iron in the dining room. Suddenly her hand jumps to her jaw; her face goes white; shock unfocuses her eyes. Her teeth had given her a twinge that started tears flowing down her cheeks as she resumed ironing. I must have cried out, for she smiled at my face. I told her she must go to the dentist, and returned to my coloring book. The comforting aroma of heated cloth folded over the glimpsed spark of pain. Now around that cold spark, isolated in memory, the air of that house crystallizes: our neglected teeth, our poor and starchy diet, our worn floors, our musty and haunted halls. I sit on the carpet—which under the dining table has retained its fresh nap and seemed to me jungle-grass—and my mother stands at the board, and around us, like hieroglyphs haloing the rigid figures of a tomb mural, are the simple shapes of the other three: my grandfather a pyramid sitting rereading the newspaper in the dwindling light of the front parlor, my father a forked stick striding somewhere in the town, my grandmother above us in her room or behind us in the kitchen, a crescent bent into some chore. As long as her body carried her, she worked.

The night we moved, my mother and I came through the wet black grass around the edge of the sandstone farmhouse and saw, framed in the doorway, close to us yet far away, like a woman in a Vermeer, my grandmother reaching up with a trembling match to touch the wick of a lamp on the high kitchen mantel. My mother's voice, in recalling that moment to me years later, broke as she added, "She was always doing things like that." Like lighting a lamp. Always lighting a lamp.

And through that "always" I fall into the volume of time that preceded my birth, where my grandmother is a figure of history made deceptively resonant by her persistence into my days. She was the youngest of a dozen children, all of whom, remarkably in that mortal era, lived to maturity. She was the baby, her father's favorite and her brothers' darling. Toward the end of her life, when hallucinations began to walk through the walls of her room and stand silently in the corners, her brothers, all of whom she had long outlived, became again vivid to her. I became one of them; she would ask for me with Pete's name. He was her youngest brother, her own favorite. His brown photograph, mounted on stiff cardboard stamped with gold scrolls, had been set up on the table beside her bed. He displayed a hook nose and the dandified hauteur of a rural buck braced to have his picture taken. Like the eyes of an icon, his snapping black eyes—alone in the photograph unfaded—overlooked her deathbed.

I believe her first language was Pennsylvania German. As some parents speak secrets in French in front of the children, my grandparents used this dialect on my mother. Only two words have descended to me—*ferhuttled* and *dopich,* meaning "confused" and "lethargic." They were frequent words with my grandmother; it is the way other people must have looked to her. Shaped like a sickle, her life whipped through grasses of confusion and lethargy that in a summer month grew up again as tall as before.

As with the blessed man of Boston, I should here provide a catalogue of her existence; her marriage to a man ten years older, the torment of her one childbirth, the eddies of fortune that contained her constant labor. The fields, the hired men, the horses, the stones of the barn and the fireplace, the three-mile inns on the road to market. The birth of my mother: the lamplight, the simmering water, the buggy clattering for the jesting doctor, fear like a transparent paste on the ceiling, the hours of pain piled higher and higher—my grandmother was a little woman, and the baby was large. Her size at the outset my mother felt as an insult ineradicably delivered to the woman who bore her, the first of a thousand painful awkwardnesses. But to me, from my remote perspective, in which fable, memory, and blood blend, the point of the story is the survival. Both survived the ordeal. And in the end all my impressions of my grandmother's life turn on the thin point of her piercing survival.

When we returned to the farm where my mother had been born, my grandmother insisted on fetching the water from the spring. In spite of all our warnings she would sneak off with the bucket and on her unsteady legs tote it back up the slope of grass, brimful, strangely little of it spilled. One summer day my mother and I were standing at the side of the house. The air was vibrating with the noises of nature, the pressing tremolo of insects and birds. Suddenly my mother's face, as if from a twinge of her teeth, went rapt and white: "Listen!" Before I could listen she ran down the lawn toward the spring, I following, and there we found my grandmother doubled up over the water, hanging, by the pressure of one shoulder, to the sandstone wall that cupped the spring on three sides. The weight of the bucket had pulled her forward; she had thrown herself sideways and, unable to move, had held herself from drowning by sheer adhesion of will until her faint, birdlike whimper for help flew to the attuned ears of her child. Death had to take her while she slept.

She never to my knowledge went outside the boundaries of Pennsylvania. She never saw a movie; I never saw her read. She lived in our nation as a fish lives in the deep sea. One night, when she thought—wrongly—that she was dying, I heard her ask, "Will I be a little debil?" I had never before heard her curiosity range so far. When presented with disagreeable information, she would look stunned, then with a glimmer of a smile say slowly, "Ach, I guess not." Wishing the obstacle away as easily as a child.

Of course, I came upon her late, with a child's unknowing way of seeing. No doubt the innocence of my vision of her is my own innocence, her ignorance mine. I am told that in her day she was sophisticated and formidable. She liked fine clothes, good food, nice things. She was one of the first women in the region to drive a car. This automobile, an Overland, spinning down the orange dirt roads of rural valleys now filled with ranch houses and Philadelphia commuters, recedes into a landscape, a woman whom I must imagine, a woman who is not my grandmother at all.

The initials were K.Z.K. Picking up that thimble, with its crown of stipples like a miniature honeycomb, and its decorative rim of five-petalled flowers tapped into the silver, I felt at my back that night a steep wave about to break over the world and bury us and all our trinkets of survival fathoms down. For I feel that the world is ending, that the mounting mass of people will soon make a blackness in which the glint of this silver will be obliterated; it is this imminent catastrophe that makes it imperative for me to cry now, in the last second when the cry will have meaning, that once there was a woman whom one of the continents in one of its square miles caused to exist. That the land which cast her up was harsher, more sparsely exploited, more fertile than it is now. That she was unique; that she came toward the end of the time when uniqueness was possible. Already identical faces throng the street. She was projected onto my own days by her willed survival; I lived with her and she loved me and I did not understand her, I did not care to. She is gone now because we deserted her; the thimble seems a keepsake pressed into my hand by a forsaken woman as in the company of others I launched out from an island into a wilderness.

Such simplicities bring me to the third of my unwritten stories. It is a simple story, a story of life stripped of the progenitive illusion, perfected out of history: the slam of a door in an empty house. "Let us imagine," Pascal invites us, "a number of men in chains, and all condemned to death. . . ."

Fanning Island is an isolated Pacific island near the equator. It now supports a relay station for the transoceanic telegraph. When Captain Fanning discovered it, it was uninhabited, but bore signs of habitation: a rectangular foundation of coral blocks, a basalt adz, some bone fishhooks, a few raised graves containing drilled porpoise teeth and human bones. All these things were old.

Understand that the Polynesian islands were populated accidentally, as seed in nature is sown. On the wide waste of ocean many canoes and praus were blown astray; short planned voyages were hazardous and extended navigation impossible. Some drifted to other populated islands and thorns there swallowed them. Some starved on the barren ground of the Pacific; some fell southward into antarctic ice. Some washed up on atolls with only the rats in the canoes still alive. A few—a very few; Nature with her mountain of time plays a spendthrift game—survived to reach an uninhabited but inhabitable island. When the company of survivors included a fertile woman, population took place. The souls shed by one nation became the seeds of another. No return was possible. The stars are a far weaker guide than armchair theorists believe. Accident, here as elsewhere, is the generating agency beneath the seemingly achieved surface of things.

What must have happened is this. A company of men in a large canoe, sailing along the Marquesas, were blown away. Eventually they were cast up on Fanning Island. They built a house, fished, and lived. No women were among them, so their numbers could only diminish. The youngest among them may have lived for fifty years. The bones of this man whom no one remained to bury moldered away and vanished. No sign of disaster is found to explain the disappearance of the men. None is needed.

Qu'on s'imagine un nombre d'hommes dans les chaînes, et tous condamnés à la mort, dont les uns étant chaque jour égorgés à la vue des autres, ceux qui restent voient leur propre condition dans celle de leurs semblables, et, se regardant les uns et les autres avec douleur et sans espérance, attendent à leur tour. C'est l'image de la condition des hommes.

—We came from Hiva Oa, and carried pigs and messages for Nukuhiva, below the horizon. My father was chief. The tabu was strong, and we carried no women in the prau. The wind dropped, and returned from another quarter. The sea grew too smooth, and lustrous like the inside of a coconut; the southern sky merged with the sea. In the storm there were lost many pigs and an old man who had seen Nukuhiva as a boy. When the sky cleared, it was night, and the stars were scrambled. At dawn the horizon all around us was unbroken; we strained to see when the great waves lifted us high. We sang to the sun, and slept in the shade of the bodies of the wakeful. The storm had torn away the hut. The cowards infected us. But the singing gave me comfort, and my father's presence sheltered me. He was the tallest and bravest, yet was among those first to yield up life. We devoured his body; his strength passed into me, though I was young. I long felt the island approaching. It gave the men hope and gaiety to touch me. The island first seemed a cloud; but Marheyo saw birds. Our sails were gone, and we paddled with hands that had lost shape. Our skin shredded in the water. Our throats had become stuck; we were silent. Two days and a night it took us to reach the island; at the second dawn its arms were reaching for us. We saw green bush and coconut palms above the rock. Before our strengths were fully revived, Karnoonoo and I fought. Though he had been a man feared in the village, I won, and killed him, grieving. We took thought to shelter. We built a house of stone, carving the soft rock, like ash, with our axes. We harvested fruit and fish, and learned to make tapa from the strange bark. We buried our dead. We carved a god from a log of the prau. We made women of each other. I was the youngest; I gave myself to those men whom I desired, the best-natured. It was not always the old who died. Demons of apathy seized Mehivi, the clown, and Kory-Kory, who had tended the god. The horizon seemed always about to speak to us; for what had we been brought here? We lived, and though we saw the others turn cold, and the jaws sink, the body turn stiff and light like a child's canoe, those who remained were not sure that they would die. We buried them with the amulets we brought from the village. Now I am the last. I buried Marheyo, the three-fingered, a season ago, and at night he speaks to me.

This is the outline; but it would be the days, the evocation of the days . . . the green days. The tasks, the grass, the weather, the shades of sea and air. Just as a piece of turf torn from a meadow becomes a *gloria* when drawn by Dürer. Details. Details are the giant's fingers. He seizes the stick and strips the bark and shows, burning beneath, the moist white wood of joy. For I thought that this story, fully told, would become without my willing it a happy story, a story full of joy; had my powers been greater, we would know. As it is, you, like me, must take it on faith.

Packed Dirt, Churchgoing, A Dying Cat, A Traded Car

DIFFERENT THINGS move us. I, David Kern, am always affected—reassured, nostalgically pleased, even, as a member of my animal species, made proud—by the sight of bare earth that has been smoothed and packed firm by the passage of human feet. Such spots abound in small towns: the furtive break in the playground fence dignified into a thoroughfare, the trough of dust underneath each swing, the blurred path worn across a wedge of grass, the anonymous little mound or embankment polished by play and strewn with pebbles like the confetti aftermath of a wedding. Such unconsciously humanized intervals of clay, too humble and common even to have a name, remind me of my childhood, when one communes with dirt down among the legs, as it were, of presiding fatherly presences. The earth is our playmate then, and the call to supper has a piercingly sweet eschatological ring.

The corner where I now live was recently widened so that the cars going back and forth to the summer colony on the Point would not be troubled to slow down. My neighbor's house was sold to the town and wrecked and picked clean by salvagers and finally burned in a great bonfire of old notched beams and splintered clapboards that leaped tree-high throughout one whole winter day's cold drizzle. Then bulldozers, huge and yellow and loud, appeared on the street and began to gnaw, it seemed, at the corner of our house. My third child, a boy not yet two, came running from the window in tearful panic. After I tried to soothe him with an explanation, he followed me through the house sobbing and wailing " 'Sheen 'Sheen!" while the machines made our rooms shake with the curses of their labor. They mashed my neighbor's foundation stones into the earth and trimmed the levelled lot just as my grandmother used to trim the excess dough from the edge of the pieplate. They brought the curve of the road right to the corner of my property, and the beaten path that does for a sidewalk in front of my home was sheared diagonally by a foot-high cliff.

Last night I was coming back from across the street, fresh from an impromptu civic lamentation with a neighbor at how unsightly, now that the snow was melted, the awkward-shaped vacant lot the bulldozers had left looked, with its high raw embankment gouged by rivulets and littered with old chimney bricks. And soon, we concluded, now that spring was here, it would be bristling with weeds. Crossing from this conversation, I noticed that where my path had been lopped the cliff no longer existed; feet—children's feet, mostly, for mostly children walk in our town—had worn the sharpness away and molded a little ramp by which ascent was easier.

This small modification, this modest work of human erosion, seemed precious to me not only because it recalled, in the slope and set of the dirt, a part of the path that long ago had led down from my parents' back yard to the high-school softball field. It seemed precious because it had been achieved accidentally, and had about it that repose of grace that is beyond willing. We in America have from the beginning been cleaving and baring the earth, attacking, reforming the enormity of nature we were given, which we took to be hostile. We have explored, on behalf of all mankind, this paradox: the more matter is outwardly mastered, the more it overwhelms us in our hearts. Evidence—gaping right-of-ways, acres mercilessly scraped, bleeding mountains of muddy fill—surrounds us of a war that is incapable of ceasing, and it is good to know that now there are enough of us to exert a counter-force. If craters were to appear in our landscape tomorrow, the next day there would be usable paths threading down the blasted sides. As our sense of God's forested legacy to us dwindles, there grows, in these worn, rubbed, and patted patches, a sense of human legacy—like those feet of statues of saints which have lost their toes to centuries of kisses. One thinks of John Dewey's definition of God as the union of the actual and the ideal.

There was a time when I wondered why more people did not go to church. Taken purely as a human recreation, what could be more delightful, more unexpected than to enter a venerable and lavishly scaled building kept warm and clean for use one or two hours a week and to sit and stand in unison and sing and recite creeds and petitions that are like paths worn smooth in the raw terrain of our hearts? To listen, or not listen, as a poorly paid but resplendently robed man strives to console us with scraps of ancient epistles and halting accounts, hopelessly compromised by words, of those intimations of divine joy that are like pain in that, their instant gone, the mind cannot remember or believe them; to witness the windows donated by departed patrons and the altar flowers arranged by withdrawn hands and the whole considered spectacle lustrous beneath its patina of inheritance; to pay, for all this, no more than we are moved to give—surely in all democracy there is nothing like it. Indeed, it is the most available democratic experience. We vote less than once a year. Only in church and at the polls are we actually given our supposed value, the soul-unit of one, with its noumenal arithmetic of equality: one equals one equals one.

My preaching fouls the words and corrupts me. Belief builds itself unconsciously and in consciousness is spent. Throughout my childhood I felt nothing in church but boredom and an oppressive futility. For reasons my father never explained, he was a dutiful churchman; my mother, who could use her senses, who had read Santayana and Wells, stayed home Sunday mornings, and I was all on her side, on the side of phenomena, in those years, though I went, with the other children, to Sunday school. It was not until we moved from the town and joined a country church that I, an adolescent of fifteen, my head a hotbed of girls and literature, felt a pleasant emotion in church. During Lent—that dull season, those forty suspended days during which Spring is gathering the mineral energy to make the resurrection that the church calendar seizes upon as conveniently emblematic —I ushered with my father at the Wednesday-night services. We would arrive in our old car—I think it was the Chevrolet then—on those raw March nights and it pleasantly surprised me to find the building warm, the stoked furnace already humming its devotions in the basement. The nave was dimly lit, the congregation small, the sermon short, and the wind howled a nihilistic counterpoint beyond the black windows blotted with garbled apostles; the empty pews, making the minister seem remote and small and emblematic, intensified our sensation of huddling. There was a strong sepia flavor of early Christianity: a minority flock furtively gathered within the hostile enormity of a dying, sobbing empire. From the rear, the broad back and baked neck of the occasional dutiful son loomed bullishly above the black straw hats of the mischievous-looking old ladies, gnarled by farmwork, who sat in their rows like withered apples on the shelves of a sweet-smelling cellar. My father would cross and uncross and recross his legs and stare at his thoughts, which seemed distant. It was pleasant to sit beside him in the rear pew. He was not much of a man for sitting still. When my parents and I went to the movies, he insisted on having the aisle seat, supposedly to give his legs room. After about twenty minutes he would leap up and spend the rest of the show walking around in the back of the theatre drinking water and talking to the manager while my mother and I, abandoned, consoled ourselves with the flickering giants of make-believe. He had nothing of the passive in him; a church always became, for him, something he helped run. It was pleasant, and even momentous, when the moment for action came, to walk by his side up the aisle, the thump of our feet the only sound in the church, and to take the wooden, felt-floored plates from a shy blur of white robes and to administer the submission of alms. Coins and envelopes sought to cover the felt. I condescended, stooping gallantly into each pew. The congregation seemed The Others, reaching, with quarters glittering in their crippled fingers, toward mysteries in which I was snugly involved. Even to usher at a church mixes us with the angels, and is a dangerous thing.

The churches of the Village had this Second Century quality. In Manhattan, Christianity is so feeble its future seems before it. One walks to church past clattering cafeterias and ravaged newsies in winter weather that is always a shade of Lent, on pavements spangled with last night's vomit. The expectantly hushed shelter of the church is like one of those spots worn bare by a softball game in a weed-filled vacant lot. The presence of the city beats like wind at the glowing windows. One hastens home afterward, head down, hurrying to assume the disguise—sweaters and suntans—of a nonchurchgoer. I tried not to go, but it was not in me not to go. I never attended the same church two Sundays in succession, for fear I would become known, and be expected. To be known by face and name and financial weight robs us of our unitary soul, enrolls us against those Others. Devil's work. We are the others. It is of the essence to be a stranger in church.

On the island the very color of my skin made me strange. This island had been abandoned to the descendants of its slaves. Their church was on a hill; it has since been demolished, I have learned from letters, by a hurricane. To reach it one climbed a steep path made treacherous by the loose rubble of coral rock, jagged gray clinkers that bore no visible relation to the pastel branches that could be plucked, still pliant, from the shallows by Maid's Beach. Dull-colored goats were tethered along the path; their forelegs were tangled in their ropes so tightly that whenever they nodded the bush anchoring them nodded in answer. For windows the church possessed tall arched apertures filled not with stained glass but with air and outward vision; one could see the goats stirring the low foliage and the brightly dressed little girls who had escaped the service playing on the packed dirt around the church. The service was fatiguingly long. There were exhaustive petitionary prayers (for the Queen, the Prime Minister, Parliament) and many eight-versed hymns sung with a penetrating, lingering joy and accompanied by a hand-pumped organ. The organ breathed in and out, loud and soft, and the congregation, largely female, followed its ebb and flow at a brief but noticeable distance; their lips moved behind the singing, so I seemed immersed in an imperfectly synchronized movie. Musical stress, the British accent, and Negro elision worked upon the words a triple harmony of distortion. "Lait eth's waadsa *cull* raio-ind . . ." Vainly seeking my place in the hymn—for without a visual key I was lost—I felt lifted within a sweet, soughing milk, an aspiring chant as patient as the nodding of the goats.

Throughout the service, restless deacons slipped in and out of the windows. Bored myself—for we grow sated even with consolation—I discovered that without moving from my pew I too could escape through those tall portals built to admit the breeze. I rested my eyes on earth's wide circle round. From this height the horizon of the sea was lifted halfway up the sky. The Caribbean seemed a steeply tilted blue plane to which the few fishing boats in the bay below had been attached like magnetized toys. God made the world, Aquinas says, in play.

Matter has its radiance and its darkness; it lifts and it buries. Things compete; a life demands a life. On another English island, in Oxford—it is a strange fact about Americans, that we tend to receive our supernatural mail on foreign soil—I helped a cat die. The incident had the signature: decisive but illegible. For six years I did not tell my wife about it, for fear it would frighten her. Some hours before, I had left her at the hospital in the early stages of labor. Wearing a sterilized gown and mask, I had visited her in a white-tiled room along whose walls gleaming gutters stood ready to drain torrents of blood. Her face, scrubbed and polished, was fervent like a child's, and she seemed, lying there swathed in white, ready for nothing so much as a graduation ceremony. She would break off talking, and listen as if to the distant voice of a schoolmistress, and her face would grow rapt, and when the contraction had passed she would sigh and say, "That was a good one," and chatter some more to me of how I would feed myself alone and who I would send the telegrams to.

Shooed from the room, stripped of my mask, I tried to wait, and was told, the comical husband of the American cartoons, to run on home; it would be a time. I went outside and took a bus home. It was the last day of March. I had been born in March, and I had looked forward to welcoming my child to the month; but she was late. We lived on Iffley Road, and around midnight, for some reason—I think to mail a letter, but what letter could have been that important?—I was out walking a few blocks from our flat. The night was cold enough for gloves. The sensations of turning into a father —or, rather, the lack of sensations; the failure of sympathetic pain, the hesitation of dread, the postponement of pride— made the street seem insubstantial. There was not that swishing company of headlights that along an American road throws us into repeated relief. The brick homes, save for an occasional introverted glow in an upstairs window, were dark in the vehement shadows of privacy behind the dry hedges and spiked walls. The streetlamps—wintry, reserved—drained color from everything. Myself a shadow, I noticed another in the center of the road. A puddle of black, as I watched, it curled on itself; its ends lifted from the macadam and seemed to stretch in a yawn. Then it became inert again. I was horrified; the shape was about the size of a baby. When it curled the second time, I went to it, my footsteps the only sound in the street.

It was a cat that had been struck by a car. Struck but not quite killed: a testament to the modest speed and sensible size of English automobiles. By the impersonal witness of the lamps burning in the trees I couldn't be sure what color its fur was—it seemed orange-yellow, tabbied with stripes of dark ginger. The cat was plump and wore a collar. Someone had loved it. Blackness from one ear obscured one side of its head and when I touched it it was like a cup. For the third time, the cat stretched, the tips of its hind feet quivering luxuriously in that way cats have. With a great spastic effort it flipped over onto its other side, but made no cry. The only sound between us was my crooning as I carried it to the side of the street and laid it behind the nearest hedge.

A sallow upstairs light in this home was glowing. I wondered if the cat was theirs. Was it their love invested in my hands? Were they watching as I pushed, crouching, with my burden through their hedge? I wondered if I would be taken for a trespasser, a "poacher"; as an American, I was nervous of English tabus. In my own brutal country it was a not uncommon insult to kill a cat and throw the body into an enemy's yard, and I was afraid that this would be taken that way. I thought of writing a note to explain everything, but I had no paper and pen. I explained to the cat, how I was taking her (I felt it was female) out of the street so no more cars would hit her, how I would put her here in the nice safe dirt behind the hedge, where she could rest and get well. I did not believe she would get well; I think she was dead already. Her weight had felt dead in my hands and when I laid her down she did not stretch or twitch again.

Back in my flat, I discovered that one glove was smeared with blood. Most of the palm and three of the fingers were dyed wine-brown. I hadn't realize there was so much blood. I took off my gloves and carefully wrote a note, explaining that I had found this cat in the middle of the street, still alive, and that I had put it behind this hedge to be safe. If, as I thought, the cat was dead, I hoped that the finders would bury it. After some deliberation, I signed my name and address. I walked back and tucked the note under the cat's body, which seemed at home behind the hedge; it suffered my intrusion a trifle stiffly. It suggested I was making too much fuss, and seemed to say to me, *Run on home.*

Back in my flat once more, I felt abruptly tired, though my heart was pounding hugely. I went to bed and set the alarm for three and read a book. I remember the title, it was Chesterton's *The Everlasting Man.* I turned off the light and prayed for my wife and, though I did not believe myself capable of it, fell asleep. The alarm at three came crashing into some innocent walk of a dream and my frail head felt like a hollow cup. I dressed and went out to the public phone booth a block away and called the hospital. A chirping voice, after some rummaging in the records, told me that several hours ago, in the first hour of April (in the United States it was still March), a perfect female infant had been born. To me.

The next morning, after all the telegrams had been managed, I went back to the hedge, and the cat and my note were gone. Though I had left my address, I never received a letter.

When we returned from England, we bought a car. We had ordered it through my parents from folders they had sent us, and, though its shade of blue was more naïve, more like a robin's egg, than we had expected, this '55 Ford proved an excellent buy. Whether being shuffled from side to side of West Eighty-fifth Street every morning or being rammed in second gear up a washed-out mountain road in Vermont, it never complained. In New York, hot tar from a roof-patching job rained onto its innocent paint, and in Vermont its muffler was racked and rent on a shelf of rock, and in Massachusetts it wallowed, its hot clutch stinking, up from repeated graves of snow. Not only sand and candy wrappers accumulate in a car's interior, but heroisms and instants of communion. We in America make love in our cars, and listen to ball games, and plot our wooing of the dollar: small wonder the landscape is sacrificed to these dreaming vehicles of our ideal and on-rushing manhood.

In the beginning, my wife and I would lovingly lave with soap and warm water the unflecked skin of the hood as if it were the thorax of a broad blue baby, and toward the end we let the gallant old heap rust where it would. Its eggshell finish grew grizzled with the stains of dropped maple seeds. Its doors balked at closing; its windows refused to roll down. But I somehow never believed we would ever trade it in, though the little girl born across the ocean in the ominous turning of April, now a vocal and status-conscious democrat of nearly six, applied more and more petulant pressure. The deal was consummated while my soul had its face turned, and Detroit the merciless mother contracted to devour her child. But before the new car arrived, there was a month's grace, and in this grace I enjoyed a final fling with my car, my first, my only—for all the others will be substitutes. It happened this way:

Dancing at a party with a woman not my wife, it seemed opportune to turn her hand in mine and kiss her palm. For some time her thighs had been slithering against mine, and, between dances, she developed a nervous clumsy trick of lurching against me, on tiptoe, and rubbing her breast against

my forearm, which was braced across my chest as I held a
cigarette. My first thought was that I might burn her; my
second, that Nature in her gruff maternal way had arranged
one of her opportunities—as my mother, when I was a child,
would unpredictably determine to give me a birthday or
Hallowe'en party. Obediently I bowed my head and kissed my
friend's moist palm. As it withdrew from the advance, her
fingertips caressed my chin in the absent-minded manner of
one fingering the muzzle of an importunate dog. The exchange
transposed us into a higher key; I could hardly hear my own
voice, and our dancing lost all connection with the music,
and my hand explored her spine from a great aerial distance.
Her back seemed mysteriously taut and hard; the body of a
strange woman retains more of its mineral content, not being
transmuted, through familiarity, into pure emotion. In a
sheltered corner of the room we stopped dancing altogether
and talked, and what I distinctly remember is how her hands,
beneath the steady and opaque appraisal of her eyes, in
nervous slurred agitation blindly sought mine and seized and
softly gripped, with infantile instinct, my thumbs. Just my
thumbs she held, and as we talked she moved them this way
and that as if she were steering me. When I closed my eyes,
the red darkness inside my lids was trembling, and when I
rejoined my wife, and held her to dance, she asked, "Why are
you panting?"

After we got home, and surveyed our four children, and
in bed read a few pages made unbearably brilliant by their
patina of martinis, and turned out the light, she surprised
me by not turning her back. Alcohol, with its loosening effect,
touches women more deeply than men in this respect; or perhaps, like a matched pair of tuning forks, I had set her
vibrating. Irritated by whatever illicit stimulations, we took it
out on each other.

To my regret, I survived the natural bliss of satiety—when
each muscle is like a petal snugly curved in a corolla of bene-
diction—and was projected onto the wrinkled, azoic territory of insomnia. That feathery anxious embrace of my erect
thumbs tormented me in twenty postures. My stomach turned
in love of that woman; I feared I would be physically sick
and lay on my back gingerly and tried to soothe myself with
the caress of headlights as they evolved from bright slits on
the wall into parabolically accelerating fans on the ceiling
that then vanished: this phenomenon, with its intimations of a
life beyond me, had comforted wakeful nights in my earliest

childhood. In Sunday school I had been struck by the passage
in which Jesus says that to lust after a woman in thought is
the same as committing adultery. Now I found myself help-
lessly containing the conviction that souls, not deeds, are
judged. To feel a sin was to commit it; to touch the brink
was to be on the floor of the chasm. The universe that so easily
permitted me to commit adultery became, by logical steps
each one of which went more steeply down than the one above
it, a universe that would easily permit me to die. The enormities of cosmic space, the maddening distension of time, history's forgotten slaughters, the child smothered in the dumped
icebox, the recent breakdown of the molecular life-spiral, the
proven physiological roots of the mind, the presence in our
midst of idiots, Eichmanns, animals, and bacteria—all this evidence piled on, and I seemed already eternally forgotten. The
dark vibrating air of my bedroom seemed the dust of my
grave; the dust went up and up and I prayed upward into it,
prayed, prayed for a sign, any glimmer at all, any microscopic
loophole or chink in the chain of evidence, and saw none. I
remembered a movie I had seen as a child in which a young
criminal, moaning insanely, is dragged on rubber legs down
the long corridor to the electric chair. I became that criminal.
My brain in its calcium vault shouted about injustice, thun-
dered accusations into the lustreless and tranquil homogeneity
of the air. Each second my agony went unanswered justified
it more certainly: the God who permitted me this fear was
unworthy of existence. Each instant my horror was extended
amplified God's non-existence, so, as the graph of certain
equations fluctuates more and more widely as it moves along
the lateral coordinate, or as the magnetic motive-power in
atom-smashers accelerates itself, I was caught in a gathering
vortex whose unbearably shrill pitch moved me at last to
drop my weight on my wife's body and beg, "Wake up. Elaine.
I'm so frightened."

I told her of the centuries coming when our names would
be forgotten, of the millennia when our nation would be a
myth and our continent an ocean, of the aeons when our earth
would be vanished and the stars themselves diffused into a
uniform and irreversible tepidity. As, an hour before, I had
transferred my lust to her, so now I tried to pass my fear into
her. It seemed to offend her sense of good taste that I was
jealous of future aeons and frantic because I couldn't live
through them; she asked me if I had never been so sick I gave
up caring whether I lived or died. This contemptible answer

—the decrepit Stoic response—acquired a curious corroboration: eventually, just as I had during the strenuous birth of my fatherhood, I feel asleep, and dreamt of innocent and charming scenes.

The next day, a Saturday, was my birthday. It passed like any day except that underneath the camouflage of furniture and voices and habitual actions I felt death like a wide army invisibly advancing. The newspaper told of nothing but atrocities. My children, wounded and appalled in their competition, came to me to be comforted and I was dismayed to see myself, a gutted shell, appearing to them as the embodiment and pledge of a safe universe. Friends visited, and for the first time truly in my life I realized that each face is suppressing knowledge of an immense catastrophe; our faces are dams that wrinkle under the strain. Around six the telephone rang. It was my mother calling from Pennsylvania; I assumed she had called because of my birthday, so I chattered humorously about the discomforts of growing old for a minute before she could tell me, her voice growing faint, the news. My father was in the hospital. He had been walking around with chest pains for two weeks and suffered shortness of breath at night. She had finally seduced him into a doctor's office; the doctor had taken a cardiogram and driven him to the hospital. He was a seriously sick man.

Instantly I was relieved. The weight of me rolled away. All day death had been advancing under cover and now it had struck, declared its position. My father had engaged the enemy and it would be defeated.

I was restored to crisp health in the play-world of action. That night we had a few friends in for my birthday party and the next day I took the two older children to Sunday school and went myself to church. The faintly lavender lozenge-panes of the white-mullioned windows glowed and dimmed fitfully. It was a spottily overcast day, spitting a little snow. While I was at church my wife had cooked a lamb dinner and as I drank the coffee it became clear that I must drive to Pennsylvania. My mother and I had agreed I would fly down and visit him in a few days; I would have to see about renting a car at the Philadelphia end. This was potentially awkward because, self-employed, I had no credit card. The awkwardness suddenly seemed easy to surmount. I would drive. The car would be traded in a few days, it had just been greased; I had a vision of escaping our foul New England spring by driving south. In half an hour my bag was packed and in my churchgoing suit I abandoned my family. *Run on home.*

Along Route 128 I picked up a young sailor who rode with me all the way to New York and, for two hours through Connecticut, drove my car. I trusted him. He had the full body, the frank and fleshy blue-eyed face of the docile Titans—guileless, competent, mildly earnest—that we have fattened, an ocean removed from the slimming Latin passions and Nordic anxieties of Europe, on our unprecedented abundance of milk and honey, vitamins and protein. He had that instinctive optimism of the young animal that in America is the only generatrix of hope we have allowed ourselves; until recently, it seemed enough. He was incongruously—and somehow reassuringly—tanned. He had got the tan in Key West, where he had spent twenty-four hours, hitching the rides to and from on Navy jets. He had spent the twenty-four hours sleeping on the beach and selecting souvenirs to send back to his parents and girl friend. His parents lived in Salem, his girl friend in Peabody. He wanted to marry her, but his parents had old-fashioned ideas, they thought he was too young. And a lot of these guys in the service say, Don't get married, don't ever get married. But she was a nice girl, not so pretty or anything, but really nice: he really wanted to marry her.

I asked him how old he was. He was twenty-two, and was being trained as an airplane mechanic. He wanted at the end of his hitch to come back to Salem and live. He figured an airplane mechanic could find some sort of job. I told him, with a paternal firmness that amazed my ears, to marry her; absolutely; his parents would get used to it. The thing about parents, I told him, was that secretly, no matter what you did, they liked you anyway. I told him I had married at the age of twenty-one and had never for a minute been sorry.

He asked me, "What do you do? Teach?"

This impressed me. My grandfather had been a teacher, and my father was a teacher, and from my childhood up it had been assumed by the people of our neighborhood that I in turn would become a teacher.

"No," I said. "I'm a writer."

He seemed less offended than puzzled. "What do you write?"

"Oh—whatever comes into my head."

"What's the point?"

"I don't know," I told him. "I wish I did."

We talked less freely after that. At his request I left him

off in wet twilight at a Texaco station near the entrance of
the New Jersey Turnpike. He hoped to get a ride from there
all the way to Washington. Other sailors were clustered out of
the rain in the doorways of the station. They hailed him as if
they had been waiting for him, and as he went to them he
became, from the back, just one more sailor, anonymous, at
sea. He did not turn and wave goodbye. I felt I had frightened
him, which I regretted, because he had driven for me very well
and I wanted him to marry his girl. In the dark I drove down
the pike alone. In the first years of my car, when we lived in
Manhattan, it would ease up to seventy-five on this wide black
stretch without our noticing; now the needle found its natural
level at sixty. The windshield wipers beat, and the wonderland
lights of the Newark refineries were swollen and broken like
bubbles by the raindrops on the side windows. For a dozen
seconds a solemn cross of colored stars was suspended stiffly
in the upper part of the windshield: an airplane above me was
coming in to land.

I did not eat until I was on Pennsylvania soil. The Howard
Johnsons in Pennsylvania are cleaner, less crowded, more
homelike in their furnishings. The decorative plants seem to be
honestly growing, and the waitresses have just a day ago removed the Mennonite cap from their hair, which is still pulled
into a smooth bun flattering to their pallid, sly faces. They
served me with that swift grace that comes in a country where
food is still one of the pleasures. The familiar and subtle irony
of their smiles wakened in me that old sense, of Pennsylvania
knowingness—of knowing, that is, that the truth is good. They
were the innkeeper's daughters, God had given us crops, and
my wagon was hitched outside.

When I returned to the car, the music on the radio had
changed color. The ersatz hiccup and gravel of Atlantic Sea-
board hillbilly had turned, inland, backwards into something
younger. As I passed the Valley Forge intersection the radio
relived a Benny Goodman quintet that used to make my scalp
freeze in high school. The speedometer went up to seventy
without effort.

I left the toll road for our local highway and, turning into
our dirt road, I was nearly rammed from behind by a pair
of headlights that had been pushing, Pennsylvania style, six
feet behind me. I parked beside my father's car in front of
the barn. My mother came unseen into the yard, and, two
voices calling in the opaque drizzle, while the dogs yapped
deliriously in their pen, we debated whether I should move my

car further off the road. "Out of harm's way," my grandfather would have said. Complaining, I obeyed her. My mother turned as I carried my suitcase down the path of sandstone steppingstones, and led me to the back door as if I would not know the way. So it was not until we were inside the house that I could kiss her in greeting. She poured us two glasses of wine. Wine had a ceremonial significance in our family; we drank it seldom. My mother seemed cheerful, even silly, and it took an hour for the willed impetus of gaiety to ebb away. She turned her head and looked delicately at the rug and the side of her neck blushed as she told me, "Daddy says he's lost all his faith."

Since I had also lost mine, I could find nothing to say. I remembered, in the silence, a conversation I had had with my father during a vacation from college. With the habitual simplicity of his eagerness to know, he had asked me, "Have you ever had any doubts of the existence of a Divine Being?"

"Sure," I had answered.

"I never have," he said. "It's beyond my ability to imagine it. The divinity of Jesus, yes; but the existence of a Divine Being, never." He stated this not as an attempt to influence me, but as a moderately curious fact he had that moment discovered about himself.

"He never was much one for faith," my mother added, hurt by my failure to speak. "He was strictly a works man."

I slept badly; I missed my wife's body, that weight of pure emotion, beside me. I was enough of a father to feel lost out of my nest of little rustling souls. I kept looking out of the windows. The three red lights of the chimneys of the plant that had been built some miles away, to mine low-grade iron ore, seemed to be advancing over our neighbor's ridged field toward our farm. My mother had mistaken me for a stoic like my father and had not put enough blankets on the bed. I found an old overcoat of his and arranged it over me; its collar scratched my chin. I tipped into sleep and awoke. The morning was sharply sunny; sheep hustled, heads toppling, through the gauzy blue sky. It was authentic spring in Pennsylvania. Some of the grass in the lawn had already grown shiny and lank. A yellow crocus had popped up beside the BEWARE OF THE DOG sign my father had had a child at school make for him.

I insisted we drive to Alton in my car, and then was sorry, for it seemed to insult their own. Just a few months ago my father had traded in on yet one more second-hand car: now he owned a '53 Plymouth. But while growing up I had been ambushed by so many mishaps in my father's cars that I insisted we take the car I could trust. Or perhaps it was that I did not wish to take my father's place behind the wheel of his car. My father's place was between me and Heaven; I was afraid of being placed adjacent to that far sky. First we visited his doctor. Our old doctor, a man who believed that people simply "wore out" and nothing could be done about it, had several years ago himself worn out and died. The new doctor's office, in the center of the city, was furnished with a certain raw sophistication. Rippling music leaked from the walls, which were hung with semi-professional oils. He himself was a wiry and firm-tongued young man not much older than myself but venerable with competence and witnessed pain. Such are the brisk shepherds who hop us over the final stile. He brought down from the top of a filing cabinet a plaster model of the human heart. "Your own heart," he told me, "is nice and thin like this; but your dad's heart is enlarged. We believe the obstruction is here, in one of these little vessels on the outside, luckily for your dad."

Outside, in the streets of Alton, my own heart felt enlarged. A white sun warmed the neat façades of painted brick; chimneys like peony shoots thrust through budding treetops. Having grown accustomed to the cramped, improvised cities of New England, I was patriotically thrilled by Alton's straight broad streets and superb equipment of institutions. While my mother went off to buy my daughter a birthday present, I returned a book she had borrowed to the Alton Public Library. I had forgotten the deep aroma of that place, mixed of fust and cleaning fluid and binder's glue and sweet pastry baking in the shop next door. I revisited the shelf of P. G. Wodehouse that in one summer I had read straight through. I took down *Mulliner Nights* and looked in the back for the stamped date, in '47 or '48, that would be me. I never thought to look for the section of the shelves where my own few books would be placed. They were not me. They were my children, mysterious and self-willed.

In driving to the hospital on Alton's outskirts, we passed the museum grounds, where every tree and flower-bed wore a name-tag and black swans drifted through flotillas of crumbled bread. As a child I had believed literally that bread cast upon the waters came back doubled. I remembered that within the museum there were mummies with astonished shattered faces; a tiny gilt chair for a baby Pharaoh; an elephant tusk carved into thousands of tiny Chinamen and pagodas and squat leafy trees; miniature Eskimo villages that you lit up with a switch and peeped into like an Easter egg; cases of arrowheads; rooms of stuffed birds; and, upstairs, wooden chests decorated with hearts and pelicans and tulips by the pious "plain people" and iridescent glassware from the kilns of Baron von Steigel and slashing paintings of Pennsylvania woodland by the Shearers and bronze statuettes of wrestling Indians that stirred my first erotic dreams and, in the round skylit room at the head of the marble stairs, a black-rimmed pool in whose center a naked green lady held to her pursed lips a shell whose lucent contents forever spilled from the other side, filling this whole vast upstairs—from whose Palladian windows the swans in their bready pond could be seen trailing fan-shaped wakes—with the music and chill romance of falling water. The world then seemed an intricate wonder displayed for my delight with no price asked. Above the trees across the pond one saw rose glints of the hospital, an orderly multitude of tall brick rectangles set among levelled and lovingly tended grounds, an ideal city of the ill.

I had forgotten how grand the Alton hospital was. I had not seen its stately entrance, approached down a grassy mall bright with the first flush of green, since, at the age of seven, I had left the hospital unburdened of my tonsils. Then, too, it had been spring, and my mother was with me. I recalled it to her, and she said, "I felt so guilty. You were so sick."

"Really? I remember it as so pleasant." They had put a cup of pink rubber over my nose and there had been a thunderous flood of the smell of cotton candy and I opened my eyes and my mother was reading a magazine beside my bed.

"You were such a hopeful boy," my mother said, and I did not look at her face for fear of seeing her crying.

I wondered aloud if a certain girl in my high school class were still a nurse here.

"Oh, dear," my mother said. "Here I thought you came all this way to see your poor old father and all you care about is seeing—" And she used the girl's maiden name, though the girl had been married as long as I had.

Within the hospital, she surprised me by knowing the way. Usually, wherever we went, it was my father or I who knew the way. As I followed her through the linoleum maze, my mother's shoulders seemed already to have received the responsible shawl of widowhood. Like the halls of a palace, the hospital corridors were lined with patient petitioners. Negro girls electrically dramatic in their starched white uniforms folded bales of cotton sheets; gray men pushed wrung mops. We went through an Exit sign, down a stairway, into a realm where gaunt convalescents in bathrobes shuffled in and out of doorways. I saw my father diagonally through a doorway before we entered his room. He was sitting up in bed, supported sultanlike by a wealth of pillows and clad in red-striped pajamas.

I had never seen him in pajamas before; a great man for the shortest distance between two points, he slept in his underclothes. But, having been at last captured in pajamas, like a big-hearted lion he did not try to minimize his humiliation, but lay fully exposed, without a sheet covering even his feet. Bare, they looked pale, gentle, and oddly unused.

Except for a sullen lymphatic glow under his cheeks, his face was totally familiar. I had been afraid that his loss of faith would show, like the altered shape of his mouth after he had had all his teeth pulled. With grins we exchanged the shy handshake that my going off to college had forced upon us. I sat on the window sill by his bed, my mother took the chair at the foot of the bed, and my father's roommate, a tanned and fortyish man flat on his back with a crushed vertebra, sighed and blew smoke toward the ceiling and tried, I suppose, not to hear us. Our conversation, though things were radically changed, followed old patterns. Quite quickly the talk shifted from him to me. "I don't know how you do it, David," he said. "I couldn't do what you're doing if you paid me a million dollars a day." Embarrassed and flattered, as usual, I tried to shush him, and he disobediently turned to his roommate and called loudly, "I don't know where the kid gets his ideas. Not from his old man, I know that. I never gave that poor kid an idea in my life."

"Sure you did," I said softly, trying to take pressure off the man with the painful back. "You taught me two things. Always butter bread toward the edges because enough gets in the middle anyway, and No matter what happens to you, it'll be a new experience."

To my dismay, this seemed to make him melancholy. "That's right, David," he said. "No matter what happens to you, it'll be a new experience. The only thing that worries me is that *she*"—he pointed at my mother—"will crack up the car. I don't want anything to happen to your mother."

"The car, you mean," my mother said, and to me she added, "It's a sin, the way he worships that car."

My father didn't deny it. "Jesus I love that car," he said. "It's the first car I've ever owned that didn't go bad on me. Remember all those heaps we used to ride back and forth in?"

The old Chevy was always getting dirt in the fuel pump and refusing to start at awkward hours. Once, going down Fire Hill, the left front wheel had broken off the axle; my father wrestled with the steering wheel while the tires screamed and the white posts of the guard fence floated calmly toward my eyes. When the car slid sideways to a stop just short of the embankment my father's face was stunned and the corners of his mouth dribbled saliva. I was surprised; it had not occurred to me to be frightened. The '36 Buick had drunk oil, a quart every fifty miles, and loved to have flat tires after midnight, when I would be gliding home with a scrubbed brain and the smell of lipstick in my nose. Once, when we had both gone into town and I had dropped him off and taken the car, I had absent-mindedly driven home alone. I came in the door and my mother said, "Why, where's your father?"

My stomach sank. "My Lord," I said, "I forgot I had him!"

As, smiling, I took in breath and prepared to dip with him into reminiscence of these adventures, my father, staring stonily into the air above his pale and motionless toes, said, "I love this place. There are a lot of wonderful gentlemen in here. The only thing that worries me is that mother will crack up the car."

To my horror I saw that my mother, leaning forward red-faced in the chair at the foot of the bed, was silently crying. He glanced at her and said to me, "It's a funny feeling. The night before we went to see the doctor I woke up and couldn't get my breath and realized I wasn't ready to die. I had always thought I would be. It's a funny feeling."

"Luckily for your dad," "all his faith," "wonderful gentlemen": these phrases were borne in on me with a dreadful weight and my tongue seemed pressed flat on the floor of its grave. The pajama stripes under my eyes stirred and streamed, real blood. I wanted to speak, to say how I needed him and to beg him not to leave me, but there were no words, no form of words available in our tradition. A pillar of smoke poured upward from the sighing man in the other bed.

Into this pit hesitantly walked a plain, painfully clean girl with a pad and pencil. She had yellow hair, thick lips, and, behind pink-rimmed glasses, large eyes that looked as if they had been corrected from being crossed. They flicked across our faces and focussed straight ahead in that tunnel-vision gaze of those who know perfectly well they are figures of fun. The Jehovah's Witnesses who come to the door wear that funnelled expression. She approached the bed where my father lay barefoot and, suppressing a stammer, explained that she was from Lutheran Home Missions and that they kept accounts of all hospitalized Lutherans and notified the appropriate pastors to make visitations. Clearly she had measured my father for a rebuff; perhaps her eyes, more practiced in this respect than mine, spotted the external sign of loss of faith that I had missed. At any rate my father was a Lutheran by adoption; he had been born and raised a Presbyterian and still looked like one.

"That's *aw*fully nice of you," he told the girl. "I don't see how you people do it on the little money we give you."

Puzzled, she dimpled and moved ahead with her routine. "Your church is—?"

He told her, pronouncing every syllable meticulously and consulting my mother and me as to whether the word "Evangelical" figured in the official title.

"That would make your pastor Reverend—"

"Yeah. He'll be in, don't worry about it. Wild horses couldn't keep him away. Nothing he likes better than to get out of the sticks and drive into Alton. I didn't mean to confuse you a minute ago; what I meant was, just last week in church council we were talking about you people. We couldn't figure out how you do anything on the little money we give you. After we've got done feeding the furnace and converting the benighted Hindoo there isn't anything left over for you people that are trying to help the poor devils in our own back yard."

The grinning girl was lost in this onslaught of praise and clung to the shreds of her routine. "In the meantime," she recited, "here is a pamphlet you might like to read."

My father took it from her with a swooping gesture so expansive I got down from the window sill to restrain him physically, if necessary. That he must lie still was my one lever, my one certainty about his situation. "That's awfully nice of you," he told the girl. "I don't know where the hell you get the money to print these things."

"We hope your stay in the hospital is pleasant and would like to wish you a speedy recovery to full health."

"Thank you; I know you're sincere when you say it. As I was telling my son David here, if I can do what the doctors tell me I'll be all right. First time in my life I've ever tried to do what anybody ever told me to do. The kid was just telling me, 'No matter what happens to you, Pop, it'll be a new experience.' "

"Now if you will excuse me I have other calls to pay."

"Of course. You go right ahead, sick Lutherans are a dime a dozen. You're a wonderful woman to be doing what you're doing."

And she left the room transformed into just that. As a star shines in our heaven though it has vanished from the universe, so my father continued to shed faith upon others. For the remainder of my visit with him his simple presence so reassured me, filled me with such a buoyant humor, that my mother surprised me, when we had left the hospital, by remarking that we had tired him.

"I hadn't noticed," I said.

"And it worries me," she went on, "the way he talks about the movies all the time. You know he never liked them." When I had offered to stay another night so I could visit him again, he had said, "No, instead of that why don't you take your mother to the movies?" Rather than do that, I said, I would drive home. It took him a moment, it seemed, to realize that by my home I meant a far place, where I had a wife and children; though at the time I was impatient to have his consent, it has since occurred to me and grieved me that during that instant his face was blank he was swallowing the realization that he was no longer the center of even his son's universe. Having swallowed, he told me how good I had been to come all this way to see him. He told me I was a good son and a good father; he clasped my hand. I felt I would ascend straight north from his touch.

I drove my mother back to her farm and got my bag and said goodbye on the lawn. The little sandstone house was pink in the declining sunlight; the lawn was a tinkling clutter of shy rivulets. Standing beside the BEWARE OF THE DOG sign with its companion of a crocus, she smiled and said, "This is like when you were born. Your father drove through a snowstorm all the way from Wheeling in our old Ford." He had been working with the telephone company then; the story of his all-night ride was the first myth in which I was a character.

Darkness did not fall until New Jersey. The hour of countryside I saw from the Pennsylvania Turnpike looked enchanted —the branches of the trees underpainted with budding russet, the meadows nubbled like new carpets, the bronze sun slanting on Valley Forge and Levittown alike. I do not know what it is that is so welcome to me in the Pennsylvania landscape, but it is the same quality—perhaps of reposing in the certainty that the truth is good—that is in Pennsylvania faces. It seemed to me for this sunset hour that the world is our bride, given to us to love, and the terror and joy of the marriage is that we bring to it a nature not our bride's.

There was no sailor to help me drive the nine hours back. New Jersey began in twilight and ended in darkness, and Manhattan made its gossamer splash at its favorite hour, eight o'clock. The rest of the trip was more and more steeply uphill. The Merritt Parkway seemed meaninglessly coquettish, the light-controlled stretch below Hartford maddeningly obstinate, and the hour above that frighteningly empty. Distance grew thicker and thicker; the intricate and effortful mechanics of the engine, the stellar infinity of explosive sparks needed to drive it, passed into my body, and wearied me. Repeatedly I stopped for coffee and the hallucinatory comfort of human faces, and after every stop, my waiting car, companion and warm home and willing steed, responded to my pressure. It began to seem a miracle that the car could gather speed from my numb foot; the very music on the radio seemed a drag on our effort, and I turned it off, obliterating time. We climbed through a space fretted by scattered brilliance and bathed in a monotonous wind. I had been driving forever; furniture, earth, churches, women, were all things I had innocently dreamed. And through those aeons my car, beginning as a mechanical spiral of molecules, evolved into something soft and organic and consciously brave. I lost, first, heart, then head, and finally any sense of my body. In the last hour of the trip I ceased to care or feel or in any real sense see, but the car, though its soul the driver had died, maintained steady forward motion, and completed the endless journey safely. Above my back yard the stars were frozen in place, and the shapes of my neighbors' house wore the wonder that children induced by whirling.

Any day now we will trade it in; we are just waiting for the phone to ring. I know how it will be. My father traded in many cars. It happens so cleanly, before you expect it. He would drive off in the old car up the dirt road exactly as usual and when he returned the car would be new, and the old was gone, gone, utterly dissolved back into the mineral world from which it was conjured, dismissed without a blessing, a kiss, a testament, or any ceremony of farewell. We in America need ceremonies, is I suppose, sailor, the point of what I have written.

TWO NEW
ANTHOLOGIES OF FICTION FROM FAWCETT PREMIER

CONTEMPORARY AMERICAN SHORT STORIES, selected and introduced by Douglas and Sylvia Angus. M359, 95¢

The best short stories from the 40's, 50's, and 60's, including the work of

Flannery O'Connor • Eudora Welty • Peter Taylor • Ralph Ellison • James Baldwin • Georgia McKinley • Bernard Malamud • Jack Ludwig • Philip Roth • John Updike • Mary McCarthy • John Cheever • Delmore Schwartz • Dorothy Canfield • Katherine Anne Porter • Wright Morris • George P. Elliott • Saul Bellow • J. F. Powers • James Purdy • Tillie Olsen • Stanley Elkin • Donald Barthelme

GREAT MODERN EUROPEAN SHORT STORIES, selected and introduced by Douglas and Sylvia Angus. M351, 95¢

Stories by the best modern European writers

Anton Chekhov • Katherine Mansfield • James Joyce • Joseph Conrad • Thomas Mann • D. H. Lawrence • W. Somerset Maugham • Jean-Paul Sartre • Albert Camus • Franz Kafka • Isak Dinesen • Isaac Babel • Alberto Moravia • Isaac Bashevis Singer • Luigi Pirandello • Wolfgang Hildesheimer • Jakov Lind • Heinz Huber • Heinrich Böll • Tommaso Landolfi • Yuri Kazakov • Alan Sillitoe • Frank O'Connor • Mary Lavin

A Fawcett **Premier Book**

Wherever Paperbacks Are Sold

FAWCETT CREST BOOKS

ON TOP WITH
THE BIG BESTSELLERS

A Fawcett Crest Reprint

Wherever Paperbacks Are Sold